SALES STRATEGIES

FOR THE ROOKIE TO

SEASONED PRO

JOE BIONDI

PAGE PUBLISHING
Conneaut Lake, PA

First originally published by Page Publishing 2022

ISBN 978-1-6624-2272-0 (pbk)
ISBN 978-1-6624-2273-7 (digital)

Printed in the United States of America

CONTENTS

WHY SALES?

WHY GET INTO sales? Work in business, finance, stocks, software, or the trades. Sales…why would you do such a thing? Or do you just think it is an easy way to make a good living?

Sales, regardless of what you're selling, is not something that will pay dividends initially. In fact, it will make you live paycheck to paycheck. It will make you question why you did this to begin with. The mental game it will play with your head will also make you question many other things about your career choice, confidence level, and test your gut to see, in fact, if you are cut out for this. So why do it?

I can tell you personally that once you do it, commit to it, and stay the course. Please commit to this book as well, and learn how to investigate opportunities, work with others, determine when to walk away, and the biggest, build relationships. Most importantly, relationships are the key! Relationships are the key, or should I say this again? Successful people in a sales role, regardless of the industry you choose, have all what I write about. So hold on, enjoy the ride and this book!

BENEFITS OF SALES

FLEXIBILITY IN A typical workday in some sales roles where you can work at night after the kids are in bed or on weekends when necessary. Sales can allow you to make an appointment with the doctor or pick the kids up at school. You usually are not tied to a desk for eight to ten hours a day. In many sales roles, there is travel, which allows you the opportunity to meet new people on a regular basis, explore a city that you typically would not visit, and enjoy some local culture. It allows you to be your own boss, as they say, determining when you need to focus and when you can breathe easy for a brief period of time.

Once you're established, it will provide financial independence to you while having the freedom to do many other things—add extra money into the college funds for the kids, take a few extra family vacations, invest in the stock market with additional disposable income, buy that nice sports car or that beach house. You get the point! It can and will happen if you're truly committed, working hard year after year and building and solidifying those relationships.

Let's say you've made your sales goals or quota for the year! Good for you! Now offer some of your time to help another salesperson meet their goals. Trust me, I've been on both sides of that scenario. Talk about a relationship builder! That partnership with someone else will pay dividends for both of you for years to come. It will also build a bond with a coworker and show that person some of your character. Many successful people end up building a client base that truly feeds them opportunities for years. Some people actually work their entire career based off a few good key customer accounts!

WHY DO YOU THINK YOU CAN SELL?

. . . .

MANY SUCCESSFUL SALES professionals I've had the pleasure of knowing and working with usually have "it." What is "it?" When you are the type of person that likes to have "the ball in your hands," you have "it." When you are cool, when it is situationally hot (I will go into detail on this later in the book), you have "it." That means that you will own the sales opportunity. It is yours to win or lose. That is why in a sport like football, it's usually the quarterback. A really good quarterback has "it." They want that ball in their hands no matter the circumstance.

You will also be the person that will drive the project by doing the research needed, coordinating resources and, having buy-in from your local leadership on what plan of action to take. Lastly, you will generate the proposal, meet with the customer, and do your best to close the deal.

Having "it" is for a special person. That means you are the type that welcomes the praise, but be careful because if you fail, you will for sure be given the blame. Just like in football, when they lose many times, it is tied to the quarterback's lack of performance. Even if in that game the quarterback played well and it was the defense, they will blame the quarterback. My point, even if that sales executive did all they could, most times they will blame sales, just a fact! However, this type of person will usually also get the praise. When someone is driven and "wants the ball," they tend to be the winning type. If you weren't raised that way, it's still possible to become that.

Of course, you will fail. The main thing is learning from failure. Recap what happened in your mind and verbalize it with others. Hold a meeting with your team members that were involved and uncover what could have been done differently. Learn so the next time it is praise, not blame! However, the failure will always be there. The competition is fierce in any industry. The customer always changes a project bid, which now puts you at a disadvantage, or a new key decision-maker was just hired, and, of course, he hates your company from past experience. But never fear failure. Respect it and keep that as a driver toward your success. Sales is not for everyone and certainly not for people that are afraid of failing. A driven person will use that fear as a motivator, not as a deterrent.

REASONS WHY I'M IN SALES

MY CAREER STARTED when I was introduced to the heating, ventilating, and air-conditioning industry back in 1992. I was an eighteen-year-old going to a two-year technical institute to learn a trade. I didn't want to be in a college classroom for another four years and sit behind a desk my entire career. I was always good at fixing things, messing around with tools, and breaking things just so I could try to fix them. Of course, I heard guys in HVAC made good money, so off I went!

We started with about twenty-five students, all but a dozen or so failed out. After my two years in school, I was the class foreman, graduated with honors, and ranked second in our class, and I was quite proud of this accomplishment. I was one of two that was automatically placed into a job with a very well respected HVAC contractor in New Jersey. I learned quickly that to earn good money, you needed to work on large commercial and industrial HVAC systems, which are quite complex—the systems that heat and cool large hospitals, universities, etc. So the job hunt began! After spending three solid years with the small contractor, I was hired by one of the world's largest HVAC companies.

While working my way up the technical ladder from apprentice, journeyman, and senior journeyman, I found myself wanting more. I spent just about fourteen years in the field and was ready for what was next. I would regularly assist our sales team in estimating projects, working with customers, and being a resource for whoever needed help. I also really enjoyed training the younger technicians and watching them grow.

I liked helping sell projects for our sales team most at this point. After all, customers listen to the technicians in the field. Many salespeople back then would just want to sell a project and make money. I actually understood why they needed to do that work and how it would benefit their building comfort, production lines, and HVAC systems. Eventually, I found out what the sales team made on projects I helped them sell, and then I was hooked. I knew at some point, wasn't sure when, but I would get into sales and be really good at it!

The year was 2006, and I won't ever forget this day. I have told this story countless times, and it always comes back to me each time clearer than the last. My wife was pregnant with our first daughter, and I was nervous and excited to become a father like most men.

It was a rainy January day, and the temperature was just above freezing. You know those days where as the rain is falling, you can actually feel it freezing on your face and hands. I had to take an emergency service call for a company that was involved in manufacturing pharmaceuticals—that rooftop HVAC system needed to be operational so they could produce their drugs. Without this system, they would lose the production of this drug due to the machinery that was overheating from the hot room temperatures. This was a critical application, and it needed to be repaired and returned to operation as soon as possible. Time is money! As a senior technician, others and I would need to handle these situations, day or night, rain or shine for the most part.

As I checked in with Carl, who was in charge of facilities at this complex, I told him I would get everything handled. Carl and I had a really good relationship. He would actually tell our account executive that managed their account to always take good care of me because I was "his guy." Again, another reason for my sales career to start, and why not? I bailed out the sales team countless times with technical issues, and I knew that it was only a matter of time for me. I just wasn't sure when it would start, until that rainy day in January.

As I went to the roof, of course, the wind was whipping around, and so was the rain. This system was of large capacity, and it cooled a significant section of their production facility. It was installed on I beam steel. So imagine this massive box about the size of a tractor trailer sitting on steel framing on top of the roof. Well, since it was raining, of course, all the steel framings were wet and icy. We all know that electricity and water don't mix! However, in order to see what has malfunctioned electrically, I had to open up the large electrical panels, which were about the size of a typical door in a house. Now remember this unit was elevated off the top of the roof about five feet in the air. Picture straddling a set of train tracks but without any wood in between those tracks that hold the tracks together which are also elevated five feet above the roof surface.

Now I was trying to lean into this panel with my electrical testing devices to see where the issue resided while straddling this wet steel. This was something I had done hundreds of times in my fourteen years in the field. This day was different—my wet boots, the wet/icy steel, the temperature or wind, or just the day my luck was to run out! I slipped and fell toward the main electrical panel! This would have been the end of my life. This machine had the electrical power of about two average homes since this was a large capacity industrial HVAC system. So basically, I was dead, electrocuted at the age of thirty-two with a pregnant wife at home ready to have our first child!

You hear people say their "life flashed in front of them" or some other saying that we always chuckle about. But for me, it's true, and it did happen. At that moment, I remembered playing with my friends as a young boy, maybe eight or ten, fishing with my grandfather, swimming in a river by our house, riding bikes with friends. I remembered being in high school as a teenager, playing sports, and finally meeting my wife. The flashback stopped right when I met her. This truly happened, and it wasn't instantaneous for me. It took some time in my brain, and the memories were quite clear.

By the grace of God or some other powerful force, I instantly grabbed the outside of that electrical panel frame and wasn't electrocuted, I was okay! I calmed myself at that moment and didn't let Carl down. I got the system back up and running, and the drug production was back online.

When I went back into the building, Carl asked if I was okay. I'm sure I was as white as a ghost. But it wasn't his usual greeting that he gave me. He knew something happened. I just told him that I was really cold and wet. He signed my paperwork, and off I went. I sat in my truck for a good thirty minutes and just stared at the steering wheel. I don't think I blinked, and as my eyes welled up, I was dazed and completely drained emotionally. At that moment, I knew there would be no way in hell that I wouldn't see my child be born or watch her grow up.

Then I knew. I did my time in the field, which I'm grateful for, and at that moment, I knew my sales career would begin one way or another!

SALES GUY IS BORN

I WAS NOW in sales. It was June of that same year, and I had made it! However, now I was the new guy again. Now I was "just" the new guy! The new guy I would say. I've been with this company for more than eleven years! The reply I would hear would be, "You're new to sales, in a new career! You are the NUG [new useless guy/gal]." Instantly, I said to myself, "Wait a minute here!" I was a senior field technician, a trainer of new technicians, and a go-to person, not anymore. Here we go again, paying your dues! But that didn't bother me too much—yeah, right!

So as each day passed, I would work with the senior sales executives and watch what they did, how they spoke to customers, how they replied to e-mails, projects, and bids. I also watched how they were in front of our customers in face-to-face meetings. I studied their every move since every man or woman as a sales executive has a different style. It was key for me to learn what I could from each one of them.

But what else do salespeople do but play golf and go to lunch I thought—yea right! It was far from that. It was everything I mentioned above, and every day, you had a plan for that day. But every one of those days, you ended up doing many other things on top of what you had planned. It was a productive day if you accomplished half of what you had set out to do! I'm lucky the people that looked out for me were top performers. I needed to be around like-minded people. They were sharp, and I was coming along nicely.

Now my account base was growing, and I had several years of sales to add to my career stats! I was making good money and being recognized as a top performer spanning several years now. I really knew I made it when we hired a new sales associate, and I was asked to train him! Yes, it was a great compliment to me and a feeling of accomplishment! And no more NUG for me! I've trained several new people over time, and I'm without question, a sales professional. The plaques of sales achievements have piled up, along with the crystal bowls and plates from that prestigious company we all know with light-blue boxes. As a top performer, that was what you were given as an award. Of course, your paycheck was compensation enough!

But learning what my strategy was took me many years, still work on that today. It always changes. It really is simple, but everyone has their own. Mine was to always be that advocate for the customer, to always pick up the phone when a customer calls. My strategy was and still is to be more responsive than the other person. I needed to set myself apart from other sellers and knew those things have worked for me. But the biggest part of my strategy is being truthful and honest—never guaranteeing something that can't be delivered or implemented, always being truthful and on every sold project, *under-promise and over-deliver always!* I've always been a large proponent of giving back. As a sales professional, I earned many awards, but I've always felt it's important to feed the future of my industry. What I mean is help generate the future. Forget about how you're compensated. Give back to your industry. Mentor someone new and volunteer to help. Be a better person than the next guy/gal. Do for others, and it will come back to you.

What I've also done is talked about our great industry at networking events, the job security it offers to talented people. I've also spoken at many career days at schools to help recruit the next generation. I've also mentored several and truly enjoyed watching them grow. You're doing this to give back most importantly, but you're also getting your name out there on a larger scale. You want and need people to remember you. It's easy to get to the top. Sometimes, it just takes some luck. It's harder to sustain that year after year! When giving back, you will obtain other connections looking to do for you. Give back to get. Simply put, invest, volunteer, and mentor, and you will get back in return—a simple life lesson anyone can understand.

ROLES IN SALES

. . . .

Sales Associates or Beginners

FOR YEAR ONE, plan on living on bologna and cheese or peanut butter and jelly! This basically means you will be broke, so don't buy anything you can't afford or take any lavish vacations!

Chase opportunities and get your name out there. Call on potential customers, follow up when they reach out for information or pricing, take them out for a morning coffee, lunch, golf outing, etc. If you're lucky, you just might sell something by tripping over it! Or that customer you start to build a relationship with may actually feel sorry for you and give you an order! Stay the course. The end result will be worth it! You are starting to pay your dues as they say.

Think of it as an apprenticeship in a technical trade, whether it be in HVAC, electrical, plumbing, or any other trade. To have any credibility in those fields, you need to spend several years (usually four or five) learning on the job and in the classroom. Until you become an actual journeyman (which means you have completed your apprenticeship), you're the butt of every joke and the one running for coffee for all the other tenured people. And whatever happens, you don't talk back or have an attitude—paying your dues, baby!

A beginner holds that title for the first few years. It takes time to build credibility and respect from peers and customers. It also takes time for you to learn your own style. You think you know yourself, but you don't in this role. When you hear "no" time and time again (meaning, we gave the business to your competitor), it will wear you down. The key is to hear "yes" (meaning, we're giving you the business) more than the dreaded "no." That "no" will make you question your decision to get into sales. It will make you question your ability and intellect as well. Again, that is stress and frustration taking your energy and focus. Understand that, know it, and strategically shift that to your benefit like I mentioned. Use that and turn it to a positive, understand that situation, stay the course, and the end result will be worth it! Get the "yes" much more than "no." As a new person, the "no" will happen a lot. Hang in there!

Prospective customers will, at times, not want to deal with someone new to sales. Don't get discouraged or hold an attitude. Understand it from their perspective and bring in an executive to help customize a solution for their needs. You can continue to be the follow-up person, the occasional phone-call person, or even the free-lunch newbie in their eyes. But the credibility and respect will come over time. What you're doing is passing their tests. Those tasks and following-up are showing to the customers that you're there to help. You're there simply to make their job easier, and you're building your reputation and integrity as a solid worker which is crucial not just in sales but in life!

When you finally get the opportunity to bid a project or service, never drive them toward a product or service they don't want or need. That will end up being the one and only sale you make with that customer. *Remember, it is the relationship that you're building for a lifetime.* Provide that product or service at a fair price. If you have suggestions for other offerings, discuss them, provide the features and benefits of those offerings, but allow the customer to decide if they make business or financial sense.

Now you will most likely hear them say something like "Please sharpen your pencil," which is a very old term used for you to lower your price. For those people, you will learn quickly about how they operate.

Next time, add 3 percent or 5 percent on top of the price you would have charged, knowing they will want to negotiate. Once they come back to you, you have that extra profit already built into your price. You win, and so do they.

A baseball reference to never forget for all your years in sales—singles and doubles. Don't swing for the fences! What does this mean? It's simple. Don't overcharge anyone...ever! Don't sell them something they can't benefit from. Now sometimes they don't know what they need, and that is your job to help guide them toward it like I've said before. But do not ever sell them something not needed. That will be the end of you with that customer once they realize they were overcharged. Let's say you hit that home run, yes! You sold them twice as many options, and they bought all of them. Big win, right? Wrong. You lost them and their future business. But yes, you did hit that one-time home run, and the payday was nice! I know some people that have made a living that way, simply dishonest in my eyes. You don't want that reputation, and you don't want to be that person, please!

Please understand what I'm saying here, pricing jobs, services, products, etc. the right way, fair price for quality product or services. That single and double will keep getting you up to the plate to take a swing. Your buddy that hit the home run, well, they traded him off. He will never again be called upon by those customers. But you, well, you keep getting up to bat, chip away, play small ball, build those relationships, price things fairly, and in the long run, you will earn ten times that home-run hitter!

The baseball reference should be read again, please. It is so important for your career in sales. I've spoken of it countless times to the newbie sales recruits. It is something that every one of them understood instantly. The reward for me is to see them mature and share that with the new salespeople joining our team. As a newbie, dig in, work hard, be respectful, call back, e-mail back, and always have a good attitude. It takes time, but hang in there, rookie. You can do it!

Sales Executives

You're now comfortable with yourself, and you know how to react in many business situations. Your book of business or customer list has grown, and hopefully, at this point, you have seen some of the rewards of your hard work. Of course, you have built relationships with your past and current customers. There is also a considerable customer base that you can call on at any time. This is typically something that you have made on your own.

But you also have learned to have that strategic vision for the future built with your customer. You can help forecast what will sell and what will just "die on the vine" as they say. Through experience, you have learned what the sales cycle looks like and have created that view from your lens. You have heard a lot more "yes" than "no" at this point, good for you!

In some sales roles, you're lucky enough to be provided with an account base or a customer list to call on. But beware of that list. You have no idea what someone before you may have done to those accounts. Always check with your office staff regarding who to and who not to call upon. As an executive, you now have built a relationship with many people inside and outside of your organization. Now when you speak about a potential project or an issue with a particular account, they are actually listening to you!

Never become complacent in your situation. Don't look at the paychecks and think, "Hey, I got this sales gig." Never take anything for granted and always continue to sharpen your skills to become an elite player in your chosen field. Don't veer off. Always stay on the course and on the road of sales success!

Never ever try to persuade someone to buy something they don't want or need. Because if you do, they will eventually realize it. Then that customer will be calling someone else. *That is called career suicide in sales!*

You must provide value, strengthen a relationship, sell as required, and deliver for their organization. The relationship you're building or nurturing will feed you and your family for a lifetime. Set yourself apart and have that strategic vision for your customer and their outlook. What are their goals? What is driving their future? What does that look like? What does that mean? An example is work with that procurement team, discuss where and what they're bidding in the future. Align your team internally. So you're ready for that project, and make your proposed solution flawless, precise, and priced accordingly. Another example is when discussing business current and future with your contact, ask what their five-year outlook is, talk about possible expansions or hopefully not reductions in size. But when you do speak of these long-term plans, show how you can and will be able to service their needs strategically as a partner in the future. If they don't have that vision, that's okay. Build it with them together. Talk about building credibility and building a relationship! You're laying the groundwork for a "yes!"

Sales Professional or Senior Account Executives

You're more than the other types of roles I mentioned. You have freedom in your day when needed. You have money in the bank, and the orders come in (or the "yes") on a regular and routine basis. The years of hard work learning and excelling in your craft have made you quite comfortable in just about every way. You certainly don't have to live from sale to sale. You're also the person that never loses focus on where you came from, never forgot the bologna and cheese days, but now you can afford the steak and lobster!

Also, as a true seasoned professional, you're looked upon by your base of customers that took years to build as their go-to person, the trusted adviser and strategic partner that makes their business pain go away and plans for the future. Never get complacent and lose focus on selling. But for every "no" you hear on occasion, a "yes" comes in time and time again shortly thereafter. Again, there is still the occasional "no," and that's fine, actually good for you since it keeps you in reality.

It is easy to slip into a fat, dumb, and happy mentality, and all successful professionals have done that at one time or another. It's not the worst thing to vacation in that for a very brief period, but don't move to that city if you know what I mean. It will ruin your career and what you have worked years to build! You also have that power within your customer's organization to help drive their business with your strategic partnership. Provide them with solutions that they need and, even sometimes, don't know they even need yet.

It is your job to customize those solutions that maximize revenue for your company, make a profit for your business, and provide value to your customer.

It is a true professional that steers their customer in the direction they feel the customer needs to go in, regardless of what you sell. This takes many years to learn. A true tactical and strategic sales professional will know how this happens. This person has done many hours of research on that customer they work with. They know how they buy, sell, pay bills, etc. This person also has relationships throughout the organization. They have positioned themselves in many areas of that company. That just didn't happen by accident. To the customer, it may seem like osmosis. To the sales pro, that was their objective all along!

Why strategically move within that organization? Think about the roots of a tree. For a tree to grow, it just starts with a seedling. It literally starts with one root from that seed. What happens if that one root or in sales, that one customer in that company you know leaves the company? Your root has died, and so have you! But if you have moved throughout the company strategically, you have built relationships and learned how to move in that organization. This is a powerful sales executive and someone that can truly keep a business pipeline growing and thriving. Meaning, this person can swing the scales for a company in a big way.

What needs to happen, and a senior sales executive knows this, is you build a relationship with that person, but at the same time, you're getting to know others within that company. You're dealing with their counterpart and others around them. Now those roots are not just one root. They're several, and the tree is growing.

This is not easy to do but is essential for success within that company you provide solutions to! As a strategic thinking professional, it takes years to master. So now how do you water that tree so the roots dig deep and wide? How do you get that tree watered? You water and make the sun shine by picking up the phone, calling them to check in, and having as much face time with key decision-makers as they will allow without being pushy. Also, you entertain them outside their office at events like coffee, lunch, dinner, ball games, golf, etc. Those roots are people. You have maintained those relationships and grew those roots deep and wide. Constant attention to their company/business is the sun and water. Now you're growing that account/customer/friend into a huge oak tree!

But always remember to covet the relationships you're building, which is obvious for many reasons. *The relationship will feed you forever if you always cherish it.* Many good customers will eventually become friends. At that point, even if they do leave that company, they will take you with them into that new company they go to.

See that, you sales pro, your friend has now brought you more business from another company. That is what I mean by the roots of a tree. Now the process starts again in another company. One root, your friend, and they will grow other roots for you. Now it will slowly become easier to build those relationships. This person becomes your sponsor (I will talk more about Sponsors later).

When the real success has hit, they will tease you about when you used to be hungry and wanted their business or how you would show up in this beaten-up old car. But the key there is they're with you. You're proven. You're dedicated to them and their business success. You're also there when they need you, and they know that. They are proud and happy for your success! After all, they're most likely a trusted business partner or friend at this point. *Always, always protect that relationship that took you years to build.* If you don't, it could be like pouring gasoline on the roots of that tree. It can die quite quickly with the wrong conversation, reply to an e-mail, or gossip. As hard as it is to grow a relationship into that, you still need to nurture it, or it will also wither away on its own. *Covet those relationships which will sustain a career!*

Do not take that relationship for granted. Remember how hard you worked to get you to where you are right now. Work even harder now to protect the business and just as importantly, if not more so, the relationship that has been built.

Business Development

This person is essentially a sales executive. These people are the ones that have to find those opportunities in their specific industry. Many times, they're networking at social gatherings, organizations, trade shows, ball games, and other areas where your industry partners collaborate.

They're meeting with prospective buyers and investigate opportunities. Once they find something that is palatable, they will partner with a sales executive to customize a solution for what their business needs are. This person must always be the social butterfly as they say. They are always doing the entertaining, lunches, dinners, games, etc. If you think it's easy, try it! It sounds like an easy job until that prospect you have been trying to bring on board all of a sudden has an issue or simply does not want to work with you. It is hard to keep customers happy time and time again. At some point, your company will fail. As that business development (BD) executive or manager, they will come to you just like they will an account executive to complain.

This person will also have sales goals to obtain. It may be by how many industry events they attend and how many new customers they bring in within a calendar year. Or they may simply be gauged on what opportunities they've found, which were quoted by someone else for that BD executive. Since many times, the BD person is not a direct seller. They are supposed to be viewed upon as essentially a relationship manager for the company. Where they can do well is when their compensation plan or bonus structure is paid on what additional revenue a new customer brings into your company. For example, if you are meeting with a customer and they sign a one-year contract with you, that can potentially earn you dollars on every job that is quoted after the deal is closed. Some incentive plans can pay 10, 20, 30 percent, etc. in a commission structure.

So for even math, your team in the next calendar year generates and sells about $500,000 in additional work from the deal you brought in. Well, your compensation plan outlines 10 percent of additional revenue credit above and beyond the contract, which is earned by the BD executive for that first year. That's another $50,000 in personal income! However, I've also seen it be very transient if the market does not require one. But a good BD executive can be vital to the success of a company. They can feed a pipeline to a sales team that provides business for years!

Just like any sales executive, their goals must be attainable. If they are not performing by bringing in opportunities for the sales teams to pursue and win, they may be looking for a new job.

HUNTER AND FARMER MENTALITY

A HUNTER IN sales is someone that closed the deal, turns it over to the office, and hunts again and again. This person is usually not interested in the long-term true business-to-business relationship. They simply have no time for that, and that is not how they're programmed or valued. They qualify and look into opportunities, strategically probe and investigate for the key buying decisions, customize the solution for that customer, propose the deal, and many times win the sale.

This is a person that is usually getting a higher rate of commission because their base salary is typically low. They know that base salary will not sustain their lifestyle. This base salary is usually just enough to keep you going. That is why you're a hunter since money is a large driver for you! Many times, this type of person is the most successful since they must hustle hard day after day. If you are, you're usually closing the most business and making a good living if you're doing it correctly.

You're just like someone hunting in the wild. You find the opportunity (the animal being hunted), you aim your weapon of choice (your proposal with a custom solution), and then you take your shot (presentation phase). If you won the work, you got your kill. If you lost the work or bid, the animal fled off deep into the forest (customer went with another company).

The farmer has a different mentality. This person is more the "order taker" or someone trying to cultivate and grow a long-term relationship with that customer. This person does all the necessary follow up, helps with the fulfillment of each sale, and deals with the day-to-day interaction. They also create a long-term pipeline of opportunities and gauge growth over time.

There is no position that is better than the other. The hunter may seem to be a more high profile. That is because it usually is. But nothing is wrong with the farmer. Think about the hunter hunting and killing without that farmer. Who would handle the day-to-day? Who would handle that business relationship? Without that being sustained and grown over time, the hunter would have nothing to hunt!

But getting back to the farmer, this person truly does know that account better than anyone if they're doing their job well. They know how this customer buys. They know the decision-makers and have relationships spread within that organization. That farmer sustains the account and strategically helps grow that customer.

In this type of role, your base salary is usually higher than a hunter since the regular interaction with this customer is much more frequent. Many times, this becomes "busy work," which are things like following up with your fulfillment team on a sold project, looking into why there are delivery delays, dealing with purchase orders or billing issues, etc. So this role has just as much non-selling as selling functions. But these are all just as important as the initial sale. If you can't invoice and collect on past orders properly, chances are that customer will not give you any additional business if dealing with your company becomes a problem. So the base salary being higher also means that the rate of commission pay is lower.

A simple example and some figures that I've seen in my experience:

A hunter where I live could make a base salary somewhere around $75,000 with approximately 10 percent commission payout for all new business they sell. So if they sell an additional $1,000,000 in new business, their commission on top of that salary could be another $100,000 in addition to your base salary. Sounds great but where I'm from, the cost of living is high! In this role, you can have years where you do very well. However, the economy plays a big factor in your success.

A farmer in the same state could make somewhere around $100,000 in a base salary with approximately 5 percent in commission payout. Selling an additional $1,000,000 in business (since they're farming mostly and not driving all new sales like a hunter), their commission in addition to that salary could be another $50,000. This role will be more of a constant since what you are selling is more of a reoccurring business. Economy always plays a part but not as much as it does for the hunter.

Just like a true farmer, they plant their crops (initial sale). They water regularly (follow-up, in-person status meetings, customer lunches, events, etc.). They watch the crops become fruitful and eventually harvested (closing day-to-day business). Then, of course, new crops are planted, and the same repeats (sustaining and building on that existing relationship).

So what are you? What do you aspire to be? My opinion is it really depends on where you are in your life. If you're new to sales and don't have many responsibilities, load that weapon and hunt once you're competent in your craft! If the seller has a family with financial responsibilities, maybe the farmer route is best, in my opinion. Maybe a mix of both roles is ideal, and many organizations are set up to do just that.

In addition, to the above types of compensation, some have a 50/50 split—meaning, half salary/half in commission *if* they make their sales targets. Their salary will be modest, but it will match the payout rate of commission as well (for example, $65,000 salary with the potential to make an additional $65,000 in commission). If they exceed those annual goals by more than 110 percent, they can get a kicker for every milestone. A brief example is if a sales executive makes 110 percent of the annual plan, a $5,000 bonus may apply, 120 percent maybe $10,000, etc.

A 100 percent commission role means you get paid when you sell—risky business for sure! That's why many people can't take that gamble! But those commission rates can be significant. You're usually on a "draw" of salary. This means, for easy math, you might make a "draw" of $1,000 weekly to cover expenses. So for that month, you drew a salary of $4,000. Since you are 100 percent commission, that is a draw of salary that you must pay back. If you make $10,000 in an eligible commission that month, you pay back the $4,000 to the company and gain an additional $6,000 of bonus or commission. Now if you didn't make that money in sales in a month, many companies that draw will carry over into the next month! You will need to pay that back once you make commissions. Be careful here. You can find yourself in a deep hole and quick! I was never a fan of this type of compensation plan.

STRESS IN A SALES ROLE

STRESS IS VERY different in how it relates to people and to what we do for a living. Stress is in every profession if it is worth anything. What I mean by that is, pay is typically in direct relation to our jobs and the stress related to doing that job. If you're not being paid what you think you're worth for the job you're doing, what's wrong? Are you proficient at what you do? Are you meeting and exceeding expectations of that job? What external forces are helping or preventing you from doing that job and doing it well? Are you stressed and frustrated because you have no control and try your best? What others do or don't do may impact your day to day and stress levels. If you simply can't help in correcting any of that behavior and you know things just won't get better, dump the stress. There are plenty of jobs out there. It's time to move on!

But first, do your research and find out what those types of jobs typically pay. If you're confident that you're doing your best, maybe you deserve more compensation either in pay, time off, or an additional company benefit. Have a nice professional conversation with your supervisor about it. Don't talk in front of others, and make sure it is in a private setting. *I can't stress that point enough!* Buy them a coffee during a break. Take them out to lunch, but let them know beforehand that you have some things you would like to discuss during that lunch so they're prepared.

Taking them away from "the grind" will only work as a benefit for you. Speak person-to-person about your concerns. But be prepared to state your case, just like you have seen in those courtroom

TV shows. Speak about what you have done well, how you have helped the company and your team succeed, what your vision is for your own career, and how hard you will work to obtain it. If you have done all this the right way, there is no reason why you shouldn't ask for more! What is the worst that happens, you hear "no," and if you do, keep yourself together and thank them for their time. None of us should feel underpaid and unappreciated for the job we do every day. Oh, and by the way, in a sales role, your boss will just tell you to go sell more to make more money. That alone is a stress point for sure!

But dealing with the stress in a sales role is crucial. Know this, you will hear "no" many times. You can spend hours and hours coming up with what you feel is a great solution for your customer. You might even spend countless hours in meetings and strategy sessions with coworkers. You might even feel the pressure of your boss when they ask if the project will be approved. That will stress the toughest of seasoned professionals. Step back, collect yourself, and keep moving forward.

When stress starts to make you panicked, overthink things, doubt your plan and solution, it is getting the best of you. Walk away from it, go have lunch, or grab a quick coffee. But keep things in perspective, remember why you're in this potential sales opportunity to begin with, and keep moving forward. When you take a step back and realize that you're overthinking and getting stressed, that is awesome! You have realized the situation, you can strategically deal with it, and now you know how to address it! Disconnecting from it for even five minutes will help get you back to the task. Identify those situations and handle them accordingly.

Some of the stress that makes people run out of sales is that damn sales quota! Your past sales are typically out there for the entire company to see. They know if you're good or bad just by looking at that data up on your company portal or a simple whiteboard. The sales executive who is at the top usually has not a care in the world for that time period. I can tell you they don't have much stress. In fact, he or she has probably taken a few extra days off, has some really long lunches, and has played some extra golf. But they will have stress.

Because once that quarter or fiscal year is over, the playing field is leveled, and it is a fresh race right out of the gate!

When you're the guy or girl on the bottom, here comes the stress, the worry, the anxiety…ugh! Why did I get into sales again? But you need to understand it and channel that energy toward the good. For example, take extra time to follow up on old projects, call past buyers, and check in. Make more sales calls in person. More face time is key with customers and continue to build a relationship. Many times, during a harmless lunch, they will indirectly tell you what they need. They might say something like "Next quarter, we need to get all capital projects proposed and submitted." (This means that all large scale bids for something you may offer would make an opportunity for you to bid.) Or they may say something like "Since we acquired XYZ Company, we now need to build out some areas within our warehouse to fit all the extra people." From there, there would be an opportunity for all building trades (HVAC, plumbing, electrical, drywall, painting, etc.). Now remember they will also need carpets, office furniture, computers, etc. So there could always be opportunity within any meeting. Again, channel the stress toward your benefit. Have it become a motivator and not an intimidator!

You can also find opportunities on the web. There are countless areas and ways to drum up business there. But most importantly, put in the extra time needed to get higher on those sales charts because, as the saying goes, "You don't have to outrun the bear, you just have to outrun the slowest person also running from the bear." What that means is, push hard every day and drive sales. Don't be the bottom man or woman. Use that stress to your benefit. If there would be any sort of company downsizing, they usually leave sales teams alone; however, if there is a reorganization, don't be at the bottom!

Quick story: I'm the manager for my daughter's softball team. Pitching in softball is intense. My daughter tried it for one season. When she didn't pitch well, I would walk out to the pitcher's mound. Of course, she already knew she wasn't pitching well. Now her dad/manager was walking out to see her. She would roll her eyes, tell me to go away, and sometimes cry! So stress got the best of her for sure.

Her career as a pitcher was very short-lived and that's ok, she is much better playing third base!

Our new pitcher was great, tough, very talented, and aggressive! However, when batters hit her pitches and got on base, she would get upset. When they scored runs, well, at that point, the stress would mount! Every time I would walk out onto the pitcher's mound, I didn't ask her to pitch better. I certainly wouldn't remind her that several runs have scored! I'd say things like "So what is your favorite ice cream?" or "What else are you doing this weekend?" or simply just ask her if she "knew what time it was" and always laugh with her, ask about going to the beach and swimming in the ocean, which she loved to do—anything I needed to do to break that initial stress I did. At that very moment, I was taking her mind away from the game for about thirty seconds. Just like I mentioned earlier, taking a break to clear your focus—returning clarity and putting her mind back on the task in front of her.

But what I'm really doing was drawing that stress and anxiety right out of her in an instant. Without fail, she would come right back mentally, pitch well, and help win the game. Our team won the division that year and were league champs with a final record of thirteen wins and two losses!

Stress—be careful with it! Be mindful of it, and always keep yourself on target, calm, and focused! Do not let it control you or your actions. It should never make you act differently also. As we all know, the damage is done once we say or do something stupid. Keep calm, stay on target, strategically deal with the situation, and harness stress for your benefit. Remember, it should be a motivator, not an intimidator!

INITIAL MEETING WITH THE CUSTOMER

WHEN YOU MEET someone for the first time, it's an immediate impression that's usually a lasting one. It happens within the first minute, less than actually. So when you meet someone, you always want to look them in the eyes, smile, and have a firm handshake. A firm grip usually relays to someone that you're assertive and confident in who you are. A limp-wristed soft handshake from a man or woman doesn't sit well with people. Of course, this is not a physical power struggle to see who can break another person's fingers—but again, firm grip, eye contact, smile, say their name, and tell them that it's nice to meet them.

That's a good way to show someone that you're credible, strong, and confident. That may not always be the case, but at least you're helping form that opinion to one that is favorable toward you. They're learning about you as much as you are them. Make the conversations based around them. A little secret, dull conversation or awkward silence? Simply look at office pictures, talk about hobbies, families, their past, education, etc. What I'm saying is quite simple. When you're meeting with someone for the first time, they will be giving you talking points everywhere you turn your head. Just open your eyes! If you're meeting with a woman that is into sports, you know this because her kid's pictures are on her desk. Her son is holding a lacrosse stick, and he wears number 16. You can say, "Oh, is that your son? He plays lacrosse?" Then just open the door and watch them beam about their child.

There is a picture of your customer with a six-foot shark. Do you think he wants to chat about that? Now it may not be easy at first. Their guard may be up. Do not come across as too pushy, keying on and commenting on everything in their space. That is just weird and creepy! You need to find your style. You need to let things look as natural as possible. What you're actually doing is learning about them and your own style. Learning about where they grew up, hobbies, their family, etc. is key for the future. Build that customer bond. Plant that seed for the big oak tree to grow!

Once they start asking about you and yours, they may not really care, but they're being respectful, or they may actually be starting to take a liking to you. That's our goal—not the sports, not the fish. Those are just tools to get things going to find common ground. You're building that relationship from a seedling! Water it and watch it grow into that oak tree! You will get used to this process as you spend more time investing in yourself in sales.

BODY LANGUAGE

....

PEOPLE CAN SPEAK without saying a word. These are the same people that may not want to do business with you. So right away, you're at a disadvantage! You meet and discuss what your company can offer. They're answering e-mails while you speak. They're taking other phone calls during your presentation or even staring out the window. In these situations, you need to keep your composure. What you can do is ask if they need five minutes to answer those e-mails or take those calls. Wait outside their office and let them finish what they need to do. Remember, you're pitching a product or service to a prospective buyer. Do not overstep and feel that you're entitled. You're not!

Now if they do take you up on that, wait ten minutes. Then ask to continue. If they can't, it's time to reschedule the meeting. Let them know that you have a busy schedule as well. Even if you have a completely free afternoon, the perception is that you're also busy and made time for them. That will sink in with the smarter people, and you really want to get that second meeting. Or they may just want to "get it over with," which isn't the worst thing. You will most likely now have their attention, but cut the presentation in half and get to the facts. Be careful here, and "please and thank you" goes a long way!

Now watch how they interact. Are they again staring out the window? Have their arms folded across their chest? Do they not make eye contact? Are they tapping a pen or their legs repeatedly? That body language is showing they're disengaged, and it's most likely time to move on. Propose what you need to propose and get out of there.

Most likely, they're taxed, due to the fact that they're overworked or have no time but need to sit through your presentation. All along, they're thinking about how much work they still need to get done. Understand that other person's day may be twice as busy as yours. Always look from the perspective of the other person.

Body language that is engaging would look like eye contact, asking questions about your presentation, open body positioning, smiles, jokes, some fun while keeping a conversation flowing. That is showing you that they're truly interested in what you're offering. It shows that you have a solution that will cure some of their business pain, which will make their lives a little easier. Nice work! That is what you need to always uncover. How is it what you're offering is going to make their lives easier. It's always about a solution to their business goals and objectives. Make their business pain disappear with a customized solution. If you have one, you propose one. If they like it, they will buy it. If they can't afford it, hang in there. It will be in the budget, and eventually, it will be a "yes."

FIND THE PAIN

....

IMAGINE FOR A second all the businesses out in the world today, all the vast industries of what makes our planet thrive and grow from a business perspective—way too many to even try to comprehend, at least for me! But in every one of those, there is pain! There are issues, delays, production problems, manufacturing issues, etc. regardless of the industry. Your job as a sales professional is to find that pain and customize your solution to fit it and neutralize it. Make that pain go away!

Here are a few examples of pain in a few different industries:

- Remember my near-death experience working on Carl's roof getting that large HVAC system back online? Well, that loss of production was anywhere from $4,000 to $10,000 per/hr, depending on what drug was being made. So they would always approve proposals for upgrades to increase operating efficiency and reliability. It was an investment in their business and a reduction in downtime, in theory, reducing the possibility of experiencing any business pain.

- Your company provides IT service support, and a large customer you deal with said "no" to an upgrade of their servers due to cost. You may simply ask what the consequential loss of revenue is to that customer when those old servers fail. What is that downtime equated to in lost revenue? If you're talking to the right person, they will know that dollar amount. Then that turnaround sell should be easy to justify by simply stating back what that loss of revenue is, and you simply compare it to the investment they're making in their business. Turn it back around to what they do and how downtime affects their revenue stream.

- Your company provides tractor trailer maintenance services, and a large food store chain said "no" to your proposal to upgrade their fleet maintenance services. Ask what the cost is to that food company when one of their trucks breaks down on the side of the road and can't deliver that full container of product. You know it will also happen right before a holiday. Justify your cost and show them in real data how much a proper maintenance program reduces downtime, increases efficiency and reliability. Then relate it to that truck being stranded on the side of the road— food rotting and that loss of revenue. In my estimation, and I'm not in the food or food service business, but it has to be in the tens of thousands for simply one broken-down truck. Again, if you're speaking to the right person, they will know that figure.

You should understand my examples and be able to relate them to what you do. That is a skill that takes some time but builds a strategic thinking sales mind. It's part of learning your craft. But once you understand it, the pain discovery will come much sooner to you each time. Like I tell my two daughters, it's all about money. It's all about return on investment (ROI), cost justification, and improved day-to-day operations. Once you prove the ROI and the value in what you're proposing, you will see those sales continue to soar! Making that ROI part of every presentation sets you apart. It makes you a strategic thinker, not just a vendor!

VERBAL BLOCKS, INTENTIONAL OR UNINTENTIONAL

THE WORDS WE use say a lot, and just like in a style of selling, you need to pick apart the negative or words that accompany a "no." These must be spun to your advantage. Here are a few examples of these words.

"They" always scrutinize every price. Your reply is "What is the decision criteria?" or "Who are they?" or "Can I meet them with you?" Is it the lowest cost or best value award? Does the CFO or someone else in authority have a brother that's in the same line of work you're in? If you think that is collusion, you may be correct. However, it is business and just how it goes sometimes. If so, just walk away and part as friends. It's a lost cause, and you're simply there for compliance reasons. Ask how long the existing company has had the business. Open the door to conversation. They will usually tell you the real reasons why they use who they do. Or "These guys we use take great care of us." In this situation, who are they? What are they like? Do you get along with them? How do they take great care of you different from other companies? Why am I here then? Why am I being asked to bid? Nothing's wrong with asking these questions, but casually in conversation, you may ask. Do not unleash all at once. Let it flow nicely!

Or the best one is "You're too expensive." Your reply could be "Compared to what or whom?" You're not trying to combat them, but *you want to win the word war to steer the "yes."* "If that's true, we can always reduce some of the offerings to fit your budget. What is that budget if I may ask?" Again, you need to drive this opportunity to closure. You're driving to the "yes." It takes time to learn and flip the dialogue, but it's a vital strategic skill to learn for your success!

Verbal blocks like "soon" or "at some point" are only stall tactics, and you need clear time lines. Ask "So what does soon look like?" or "At some point is approximately when?" You're not trying to be pushy, but you must get clarification. This way, when that time is up, next week or next year, whatever it is, you have earned the right to follow up. They're not your words that you're following up on. They're the words of the customer that you're following up on.

The best one is we "can't" do this work right now, or we could "never" get this project approved. Your reply is "What if you did the project? Imagine what a relief that would be." Have them envision your product or service already in use. Speak about the operational savings and reliability it will provide, reducing their business pain! Then justify what solution you've provided to conclude that this vision can be a reality if they move forward. Not "can't" but maybe next quarter or before the end of the year. Don't make it a definitive "no." Open the possibility to "soon or maybe." At least you still have a "possibility" and not walking away altogether. Spin, spin, spin the negative to a positive. Win that word battle! This takes time, but it is a crucial tool required in your sales tool belt for success!

As you have the time to present your offering, let the hard work you have invested speak for itself. Don't say things like "I can offer this today only," "This sounds like a great deal, doesn't it?" "You know what we are trying to sell will work great for your company." Those terms died many years ago. They're actually labeling you as a "salesperson" and putting you in the same category as everyone else that "sells." You want to be that strategic solutions provider and that consultative person that has a vision for that company and your relationship with that client. Find that pain, consult with them on a solution, and offer to make it go away. That will make a person go from vendor to adviser.

ATTITUDE AND POSITIVE THINKING

· ·

YOUR ATTITUDE WILL drive you, good or bad, just like stress. You have to look at each day with a positive outlook and a good attitude. We all have things or bosses making us do what we don't want to do at times. It's important to do what you need to do and keep a good mindset. How you view an opportunity in sales can and will drive your performance. That alone is a very strong strategy to keep with you in a sales role.

For example, you might say, "Why do I always get the bottom sales leads that come into our office?" That will automatically make you look at a situation negatively. What you could say is "I'm getting another lead from my sales manager!" This is now another opportunity to plant a seed! Don't look at just that one small opportunity with a price tag on it. Think of it as another person you will go out to meet and another company that you will get exposure with!

Always remember that someone may be talking to you, and they have issues at their house, job, with their kids, etc. You don't have any idea what kind of morning, week, or month they have been having. If a customer or prospect has an attitude with you and we all know what that sounds like, keep your composure and don't take it personally. You are the pro here! Ask if they would like to speak or meet at another time. You can carefully even say something like "It sounds like you may be a little upset right now, and I want to respect your feelings." Then you can offer to reschedule your meeting. If they weren't upset and that is how they talk, it isn't the first time they have heard that. If they do take your offer and do reschedule, I can assure you that you have just built some credibility. Again, be careful in this approach. Please and thank you as well are needed. This approach will work, but use it carefully!

Any one of us can have a bad day at times, completely normal. But always drop that at the door to your office. It is game time now! Drive hard for what you need to propose, call those customers or prospects back, talk to your coworkers, laugh, and turn that bad morning into a positive and constructive day for selling! If you simply can't manage that, take the day off. That bad attitude or bad way of thinking can do damage with coworkers and customers. You always need to be ready to play. You always want the ball, but the mind game must be won—a positive outlook and a good attitude every single day!

The people around you can also play a big part in your attitude and thinking process. If you're always going to lunch with that fellow sales rep that just complains about how they lost a big deal, they complain about how they have missed their monthly or annual sales goals, they talk poorly about the boss, coworkers, and customers, stay away! This person will certainly drag you into the mud, and they hear plenty of "no." Just like a chicken, they peck all around on the ground with one another, all doing the same thing with a pack mentality. Complain and blame—that is what they do best since it surely isn't selling!

Spending time with people that have a positive outlook and good attitude is what you want—usually seeing the good, working well with others, laughing, enjoying their day and one another. This is someone that is soaring high in the clouds just like an eagle. If you have ever noticed, that is where they typically live—way up high where no predator can reach them, up in the clouds, soaring higher than any other, not pecking at feed on the ground like a chicken! Eagles usually hear a lot of "yes."

It's also important that you and these people are sharing the same strategic vision and have that same outlook. What I mean here is speak with fellow sales executives about opportunities and brainstorm. Discuss some of the details of a bid or project. Get their feedback and see if your vision is like theirs. Maybe they see things differently, which may provide a specific angle for you and help you sell. Maybe they can provide other examples of what has worked for them in the past. Collaboration and teaming of like-minded sales pros is quite powerful! You all must want to win. (Believe it or not, some people don't really care if they sell and are okay with being a bottom-feeder—stay away.) You all must be aggressive, assertive, want to do right by the customer and the company. They also must value and covet relationships as you do. That is why it's very important again, to be with like-minded sales professionals that have that same strategic vision.

I can't stress enough here. Soar high, empower each other, and fuel yourself and your team mentally. This mindset will spill into all aspects of your life, whether it's encouraging your spouse to get that new job or reassuring your child that they can win that big part in the school play! How you interact with people isn't just day-to-day interactions. It's part of your legacy—how people view you, how they will remember you, and what stories will be told of you. Would you want someone to say that you were difficult and always had issues? Would you want them to say you were always nasty at home with family and friends? Of course not, and believe me, I struggle at times with this. But I always try my best, and people that know me know I do. We're all made differently, and no one person has it all. But to break apart someone on any level only hurts their spirit and tears you down as well in their eyes. So be known and remembered as that eagle soaring high, empowering, helping, and encouraging!

I have a customer that is a director of facilities for a large company that makes food additives. He has a team of people that report to him, and he does quite well for himself. However, this man came from nothing. When he was a child in El Salvador, his grandfather had a large storage hole underneath his floor. When the banditos would come to his village and kidnap/recruit the next generation of gang members, he would hide there in that hole under the floor. Finally, his grandfather put him on the back of a cargo train and told him to get to America. At the time, my friend was all sixteen or seventeen years old. Eventually, he did. He started out digging foundations for houses, didn't speak the language, and had no money but made enough to rent a bed and feed himself.

Along the way, he met people that empowered him and encouraged him to advance himself. He learned English, worked hard, and he was a good citizen—thank goodness! This man is a person that I'm glad to call a customer that became a good friend. He is quite thankful for what he had worked hard for. But his path in life brought him up with the eagles! His story is truly what movies are made of. He now does all what is good in people, provides guidance, helps, volunteers, mentors, gives back, and lives as a good person. Your story could be worse than his. It doesn't matter. The decisions we make every day and how we choose to interact is up to us!

APPEARANCE AND DRESSING LIKE THE CUSTOMER

. . . .

THE OLD SAYING is to "dress for success," which is true, somewhat! Of course, you need to be presentable and look like a human! If you haven't shaved or combed your hair in a week, that could be an issue! You need good hygiene—shower, trim the beard, or shave closely. Keep your hair somewhat styled, or if you are like me, comb whatever is left! But your appearance will communicate with your prospect or customer before you even say, "Hello, my name is…"

The dress code should always be professional. It never matters what you sell! You must wear a clean button-up shirt and pressed pants. Or if you're a woman, a nice business suit or shirt and pressed pants. Shoes should always be clean and presentable as well. If you wear boots of any kind, keep them tied and also well kept. If you think for a second a prospect or customer of yours doesn't notice these things, think again. As the saying goes, "The first impression is usually the lasting one!"

If you look like a beaten, tired, wrinkly, and simply a scruffy mess, please don't get into or stay in sales! This is simply not a role for you! The attire does not have to be extravagant or have a designer logo. But it must be clean, match, be wrinkle-free, and, of course, free of pulls or rips. The person that keeps themselves together is the person that appears professional, organized, and intelligent—believe it or not! The perception of the wrinkly, scruffy person is simply lazy, down on their luck, and unsuccessful. The key is to always look the part regardless of your current situation. Dress for success every day since successful people attract successful people!

The way your customer is dressed should not be outdone by your outfit. Never ever do this! Who would think these things matter? But they do. If your customer wears very casual attire or even jeans, stay with your casual business gear like I mentioned. For ladies, also like I mentioned, if your customer is a man and wears a suit, it may not be a bad idea to match him. Again, you will appear to be successful, organized, and a professional, which they will be attracted to, someone like themselves.

You should get the idea from this point, but here is a real simple way to remember it. If you look overdressed in your customer's eyes, they will think, "Wow, he/she dresses very well. Maybe they're overcharging me." If you look like a tired, wrinkly mess, they may say to themselves, or worse, their peers, "Did you see how they were dressed with the rip in his/her shirt that was wrinkled? I guess they don't have much success and maybe can't afford a business wardrobe."

People want to do business with successful people. If you think I am wrong, you are. Trust me! A customer will judge and analyze you as much as you will analyze the opportunity in front of you. Be careful with the flashy imported car. Be ready to defend that choice of vehicle. If you pull up to a customer's business driving one of those, the first thing they will think is *I'm getting overcharged. Look at the car he/she is driving*. It is a fact and human nature. My suggestion is to keep that high-end vehicle at home and drive a "good ole reliable" to work and customer visits. It does matter, even though you may be laughing right now. It matters. Yes, it's a game, but you must play!

BE THE MEETING LEADER

SET THE AGENDA and stick to it. What this means is make sure that your customer knows that spending time with you is valuable and will be mutually beneficial. Always have a script so they know what will be accomplished during your meeting. What I would do a day or two before the meeting is e-mail out an agenda—simply written similar to one of mine below:

> *Hello, XXXXX (if you are on a first-name basis only!), or Hello, Mr. or Mrs. XXXXX,*
>
> *Thanks again for setting aside an hour to meet with me tomorrow. Below I have my meeting agenda outlined:*
>
> 1. *Introductions (if needed) along with roles and responsibilities*
> 2. *What our team locally is doing well*
> 3. *Where we need to improve*
> 4. *The escalation ladder within (insert your company name) and who to contact in times of need*
> 5. *Discuss open items or progress report on a current project (optional)*
> 6. *Discuss unpaid invoices and/or aged financials (optional)*
> 7. *How and where else we can help support (insert their company name)*

8. *What are the long-term goals this year and/or next year for (insert their company name)*

Of course, your pressing items will override my agenda, but I think we should be able to cover what's listed above within the one-hour time frame set aside.

See you soon!
(Insert your professional signature along with company logo below)

Now you have made the agenda for the meeting and set the time line. This will start to set you apart from your competition and not just another vendor. When you discuss their business, your company, and how we're currently supporting them and their business, along with their vision of the future, it puts people in the position of a strategic partner and not a vendor.

In this meeting agenda, some key takeaways are number 2, I am concerned how my team is performing for you locally (not selling), number 5, I want updates on current projects (not selling), number 6, I want to make sure if there are any issues with payables or receivables that I'm here to help rectify projects that are currently in motion (not selling), and the biggest of all, numbers 7 and 8, the vision! The vision! That is it—where are you going in the future, what are those long-range plans, and how we can go down that road together. You are the true strategic partner here, not a vendor! Yes, that is the sales piece and what is backfilling your pipeline of opportunities! All those agenda numbers, they're good solid talking points. Of course, you need to sell. But you're watering and planting new seeds at the same time. You're managing the account activity, assisting with deliverables, and looking to the future. Sounds like a real sales pro to me!

Remember, as you start to show this customer your business plan and how you can help them, it will open doors. People are way too busy in the climate we all work in these days. They will, over time, welcome you to help drive their vision and comply with what they will need. Whatever your business is, they will find the need and truly give it to you. The position you build for yourself will pay dividends. It will allow you to take that away from your customer since they know you will handle it. You understand their business model and understand their vision—in hopes that you built that strategic platform together. But for them, you're taking some of their business load off their shoulders. That's okay. It's your business, driving you forward to your sales and profit quota!

The most important thing to remember here is to always help solve their issues or position yourself as their consultant, not a salesperson. But during your meeting, if you have follow-up items, such as to provide technical data, get it and send it or stop by on your way home and drop it off at their office. If you need a subject matter expert to meet with their subject matter expert, follow up and coordinate that. Do what you say you will do. At the end of the meeting, repeat the "action items" so everyone understands who is doing what, assign roles, responsibilities, and time lines for completion. I can tell you that over time, your competition will fade away, and your sales within that account will rise. I've done it several times, and yes, I do speak from experience. Be that consultant, strategic partner, and visionary, not a low-bid vendor that only sells to price. Too many companies are driving to price-based decisions. Be the one that's different! Prove that value does have a cost. Spend that time to customize your offerings, make it be an easy sell, and have your customer sell it for you. You found the pain. Your solution will reduce and minimize that pain. Now have the solution sell itself! Ask for the business. You've earned the right. Get that "yes!"

BEING COOL WHEN IT'S HOT (COMFORTABLE WITH THE UNCOMFORTABLE)

THIS MINDSET TAKES time to learn, understand when it occurs and how to channel it. This chapter is all about the example, which will make you get it and quickly.

For example, our product or service is delayed or missed a deadline for production. That, in turn, makes your customer that bought from you look very bad to their superiors. Now he/she is in trouble. So what do they do? Of course, they call you.

If you're lucky, you just get yelled at over the phone, but many times, these conversations or verbal beatings are face-to-face. So when they're venting, yelling about a production line, assembly line, missed service you were to provide, etc., it is very important that you keep your cool here. You're the sales executive they bought from. They don't want to hear about some strike your factory had in another country, the boss that was out sick and couldn't approve the order, etc. It's on you. Own this situation, and it will build respect in the eyes of your customer.

I've been here many times due to external forces. Hold on and keep your cool. Don't blow it and react without thinking. When a situation is heated, remember this, many are looking for you to engage and fuel the situation. *Do not* fuel it by providing an excuse or a reason as to why you couldn't comply with the agreed delivery date. No excuses and don't be, in any way, visually annoyed. Body language is key in this situation! *If you are, that will be the best way to lose that customer forever.* That will never be forgotten if the situation is big enough. Being visually annoyed, looking away, pouting, holding your arms across your chest, looking out the window, etc. displays to them your lack of interest or attention to this serious matter. It would show me that you're just not seasoned enough to handle a difficult situation!

Let them vent or yell as needed. Sit there as a professional and try to understand it from their perspective, as I said earlier. What issues will they now have? What will their boss say? Always remember they do have a right at that moment to be upset. They chose your company, and your company failed them. *I could care less if you had nothing to do with the failure. Get used to it. It's sales! You're the sales executive. You eat it! It is your relationship that's in jeopardy!* Be mindful of your body language, and, of course, the words you choose. Apologize, listen, repeat their concerns, follow up with your office on those concerns, and you must return to that customer with an update. No update at that moment? That's okay then return that call, return that e-mail, and say that you're still waiting on that update. Silence and going "dark" in that time of need is another way to lose that customer. In these situations, overcommunicate so they see you're there in good times and bad. You're building your own personal character and armor for situations like these. Over time, they become less uncomfortable for you personally.

How you bounce back or stay cool will speak volumes of you in their eyes. Of course, you need to deliver on what was sold! That goes without saying. But again, your reactions, your interactions, your behavior at that moment can make or break that relationship forever. Know the situation, know your customer, know what they're dealing with. Listen, stay engaged, follow up, and execute! See comfortable with the uncomfortable—piece of cake!

LOUD (Listen, Observe, Understand, and Deliver)

This acronym is what I've used for countless years in difficult situations, and here's how they work:

Listen—listen to the issues of who did what, why this happened, who said what, what the consequential damage is, etc. Listen to the story very closely and even ask if it's okay to take notes. I always pulled that move, and an upset customer loves it! They see you're engaged in finding a resolution!

Observe—might be the biggest one to remember in LOUD. In this situation, you will be hearing things that you will not typically want to hear. Watch your behavior like I mentioned earlier. That's the eye contact, attention to their detail they're sharing, your arms—are they crossed and holding yourself tightly, showing that you're taking offense? Are your legs twitching and tapping constantly, showing signs of nervousness. Observe yourself like you're sitting across from yourself, watching your own reactions. This is something you really need to master over time! Keep yourself together, keep eye contact, understand what they're saying, and be the professional I know you can be. It isn't easy taking a verbal beating. Watch your reactions closely.

Understand—if you were in their position, would you be just as upset? Would you be even worse? Remember, they chose you and are most likely having some buyer's remorse right about now. Understand all what they're saying from their perspective.

Deliver—now you have to make that message clear and perfect. How you react in this situation might be a make or break point! Your words at this very moment are pivotal. If you can't formulate a good message at that moment, you need to get out of there. You can say something like "I've taken many notes and heard all your concerns clearly. I will need to go back to the office and speak with management." Now in this scenario, you have devalued yourself. You have basically told that customer you have no authority and need to go home and "ask Mommy." Not a good position to put yourself in. *But* that approach might be better than opening your mouth and digging a deeper hole. If you choose this option, get back to the office, speak with management, and get them an answer the same day, no exceptions. Let them see this is just as urgent to you as it is them, and you're all in it together.

You want to provide some clarity in this situation. You need to have the back of both your company and the customer. But I never said this game was easy to play! Sympathize with your customer and provide insight into the situation even if the issue relates to things that are clearly out of your control. Preface it with something like this "I know we didn't hit the production deadline, and it put you in a bad spot with the manufacturing team and your leader. I'm sorry for that, and the reason was that our team oversees had a major power outage that took us offline for two days" or "I know we missed the deadline by a week, but the trucking company delivering our raw materials had an accident which put us off track by several days." *It is never an excuse and makes that clear; however, it is a justification of what happened.*

SOMETIMES, JUST SAY NO

CUSTOMERS ON A regular basis need to go out and obtain pricing from other companies for the same things that you currently offer. (I did go into this briefly earlier, but it's important to outline again.) They need to do this for various reasons—a compliance agency, MOP (method of procedure), bid requirements, or just for some other reason the boss needs to give them another task to complete! But remember this always, salespeople are typically paid off results. So where you spend your time is crucial since the hours in the day need to work toward your sales goals and the goals of your company.

If you get a call from that same company year after year to help them with their capital money to obtain from corporate, if you help them reduce their operating or maintenance budget by revising a proposal for the third, fourth, or fifth occurrence at this point, you're spending time. They, in most cases, could care less! You're helping them do their business, and you walk away with nothing. Like I said earlier in the book, it's time to move on from that account or customer—another price check for another year. Next year, they will perform the same exercise with you. In the future, like the chapter says, it is okay to say no! How we relay that information takes professionalism and respect, of course, but it's okay at times to tell a customer you're not interested.

Leadership many times will stand behind this decision since they also want you to work, to sell, and to drive toward your goals and the goals of the company. The boss usually gets a bonus based on your individual results. So they will also be mindful of where you spend your time. Make the boss the bad person that says, "We as a company are no longer interested in these bids and rebids." They will know how to answer professionally. If your customer has any understanding, they will also know that you've tried to help them for a few years now and no longer can assist. The only thing you have earned with this customer is the right to walk away without their protest.

In theory, I would hope they just call someone else. That does sound insane, doesn't it? We want that customer to call someone else. Yes, we do! The exercise of price, price again, and price a third time means a few things—they don't know what they want, they want you to tell them what they need, they want to use your expertise as a free consultation, or a combination of all the above. Move on and work with customers that want to work with you. Slow day, not much on your agenda…perfect. Stop by a key customer or two, say hello, take them for lunch, and just shake a hand. That shows them that you're there. That's again the water on the tree, making it grow!

TAKE AWAY HOME-FIELD ADVANTAGE

MANY CUSTOMERS THAT are in charge of procurement, oper-ations, finance, etc. spend many hours during the day in the office. Like many of us in today's business climate, it's a long day—countless conference calls, e-mails, reports, presentations, and financials. So with people such as these, their office becomes like a second home. They may spend forty to sixty hours in that same office behind that same desk. That is their home field, and you're the visiting team.

When a project is being bid, they have the advantage since they have written the project that's out for pricing. If you have that strategic partnership already built, you have the advantage since you helped design this bid! They already have a budget in mind, and they know who will be coming in to propose and potentially win the work. All the estimating time, research, and meetings you had to propose this, and now you're the visitor, and they have home-field advantage. Remember, this office is a second home.

Do your best to get them out from behind that desk. Level that playing field! Make it a neutral field, court, or arena, depending on your sport (yes, that is a joke). Here is how we, as sales professionals, do this. Ask them to take a walk while you talk about the project. Ask them to show you the area where the component or system will be installed. Ask them to get some fresh air for five minutes to discuss it and get in a few steps. Best of all, do it over coffee or lunch. They can't get away, not a problem and simply order in a pizza. Grab a spare conference room for fifteen minutes to eat together. It works. Just get them away from the desk!

When you neutralize the dominance, you make it more personal. You walking into their office on their home field, you're already at a disadvantage. When you make it a neutral environment, they will be more receptive and willing to help. It's human nature. As people, we truly do want to help one another. What better way than to provide business to people we like. It is totally normal and good business.

Just remember what I'm saying, level the playing field.

The Presentation Day

How many people love to stand in front of a room and have all eyes on them? How many people want to be asked questions they may not be able to completely answer? How many people enjoy the stress of preparation, making slides, dealing with the research, and practicing presentations? If this sounds like a miserable job, it is! But it's part of the final stages of sales and business and in many situations, something that needs to be done.

Here is a little secret. In business, everyone is afraid of making a decision or certainly the wrong one! That's why procurement people ask for a company to come in and have a presentation on what you're trying to sell and, of course, what they need. So it's important that you consult with your team on who will own what parts of this presentation. You must have role clarity, and everyone on this team knows what they will do.

Some examples of people that you should have on your team for the presentation are the following:

1. The face of the company (usually the sales professional that has gotten you to this phase)—they're typically the one that will present in front of the room of decision-makers. This person will be the intelligence gatherer as well afterward. They must have a good enough relationship with their point of contact from the buyer's side to tell you how you really did on the presentation, what they liked and

didn't like, and what the inner circle of decision-makers are thinking, crucial step!

2. You need an SME (subject matter expert) which will provide technical input on an as-needed basis. I love all technical people, but many times, they don't know when to A, keep quiet, B, simply start talking, or C, which is the biggest of all, when to tell the salesperson to stop talking since they're saying something wrong! One thing good salespeople do is talk to carry a conversation! So the SME must add technical data to keep everyone whole on what your product/service can do.

3. You must have a decision-maker from your company! This is the person that can approve or decline an audible! What is this "audible"? It means this person handles the side deal or the "make or break" moment. If the presentation is at a standstill, this person makes the deal happen at that moment. If the customer does want your offering but is stuck, this person can help sway and approve the decision at that moment which allows your team to leave that meeting with an order. What you don't want is time to pass, which allows the competition to creep back in and take your deal! So the decision-maker can approve an expedited production time line, expanded product/service with no additional cost, or rebates based on quantities ordered. *What did we "not" do…simply lower our price!*

3a. The same person that's the decision-maker is usually the timekeeper. If you have an hour for a presentation, they need to make sure you're on track. This usually happens when the sales professional who is presenting does a dry run with the team listed above. They should pretend to be that customer. Have objections for the salesperson to answer which is a very good way to rattle a presenter. Make sure they interject some questions or comments while the presenter is speaking. That will throw off their mindset, and that's what you want. This is practice for the presenter to prepare for what may happen. Then the timekeeper knows how the cadence is, how long each slide should take, and what's left to cover in the allotted time. The presenter needs to be in visual communication with the time-keeper. Maybe a tug on the right ear tells the presenter to speed up or slow down.

Having done many presentations and training classes myself over the years, you need to be ready for that situation "on your feet." But good sales professionals don't get worried about things like that. Nervous energy, yes, and that's okay. You can call them pregame jitters which all performers should always have. At this moment, that's what you are, on a stage to win or lose the deal! Like I said earlier, you "want the ball" in your hands! I've always thrived in those situations and welcomed them. Many talented people I know also feel the same. I'm not boasting. I just know my strengths and weaknesses equally.

Embrace the uncomfortable. That's when you grow as a professional. Get out of that comfortable little nest and fly out. You will fly or crash to the ground. Good comes from both, and here is why. When you fly, you gain confidence in your ability and as a professional. When you crash, it shows you where you need to improve and what you need to work on for next time. Don't ever stop trying again. This is part of what good sales professionals do well.

But during the presentation, as the lead point person for this opportunity, keep a casual eye on your internal team while you're standing in front of a room of decision-makers and fellow team members. That key person will give you that pre-orchestrated sign if you're on track. Or they will also provide the sign if you're veering off the road. The main thing is to be comfortable at this moment. It's "game time." Your presentation is what will most times make the deal. It may not matter if you offer the best product or service. If you can't relay the company message properly and clearly, you have lost momentum and many times, have lost the deal.

Be comfortable. Don't "ah or um" yourself to death! Have a key person on your team monitor those useless words. In times when we're speaking, we feel that dead air needs to be filled in between sections or presentation points, but they don't! Just let the time go silent. Your words will mean more in that moment of intentional silence. If you're doing too many of those types of things, have your team member give you a rub of their nose or some other covert sign. Or better, each team member can have an "ear tug" for another reason—the "ah or um," the "time is running out," the "stop flailing your arms," or any other "tick" that you personally have. That's why you have the practice presentation!

It isn't easy to be the presenter, but this is one of the biggest parts of being a strong sales professional! The victor gets the spoils and usually the nice payday! Keep yourself on track, watch your tone, increase it, and decrease it at times intentionally, which usually keeps the engagement of an audience. Stick to what the objective is. If you need to provide an example of another project that you worked on in a similar fashion that will help prove a point of your presentation, do it. Keep it very brief. This time and in this moment, it's all about XYZ Company. Don't spend more than a few minutes talking about ABC Company. Also, do not reference that other company by name. Just say, "Another company that's similar to yours," or simply, "Another project I worked on."

YOU CLOSED THE DEAL, NOW WHAT!

WE ALL HAVE said, "Uh-oh," once that presentation is flawless and that large project sells. Heck, you may have said to yourself, "There's no way this will ever sell," and then you have an order. You got the "yes!" I can tell you with certainty the supplier, vendor, or manufacturer you called for pricing for the original bid will now have experienced many pricing increases since you bid that project, product, or service—which in many cases is what happens.

Costs for everything do go up, along with salaries, benefits, office expenses, etc. Or maybe the prices quoted to you when the project was initially bid have somewhat maintained a level, but you don't know this, of course. Then that's just a way for that vendor to make a higher profit margin on whatever your team submitted a bid for utilizing what they will sell you. Have that vendor honor the price they gave you from back then if at all possible. It will be somewhat uncomfortable for you to request this. But either you gain higher margin on what you just received an order for or your vendor will take it, knowing you need what they sell in order for you to execute on what you just sold. Confusing? Sure is.

Flip the script, and here's how we do it! You now have the customer's order. Call that supplier back and tell him that you're close to winning this project (even though you have the signed contract or purchase order). Have them reduce some pricing if possible and then call the vendor back the following day and thank them for revising the price and say that you won the job! This is not an unethical business practice. This is having your commission increased and also having the company see more revenue. Either you take it, or the vendor will take it from you! It's a game and takes time to do, but it will become part of your craft once you get used to it. Do not do it on every single order—just the significant deals.

Next, your management team that originally gave you a thumbs-up said, "Go get 'em," will now have amnesia and swear that you never discussed this project, and lastly, the customer will want to know how soon you can deliver. Not only deliver at the agreed time line but also how much earlier you can deliver. These are issues that all sales professionals deal with. Remind your manager of the meetings you had, even forward the e-mail interactions back to show them they did agree to this. Tell the customer you will do your best, but that's why you both worked out an "agreed" time line—expediting it, wishful thinking, yes, but not something you can deliver with confidence. Demanding expedited shipping can result in poor manufacturing quality, and make sure you remind the customer of that. Continue to stay engaged since you now have to deliver on what was sold. After all, you can always get lucky and trip over a sale. That isn't the issue. It's the delivery since you will also be the point person. If you can't deliver and comply with a time line, would you call yourself back for another product or service bid? Of course not! Like I said, it's a little hot. Stay cool, my friend!

Now the execution of the product/service is just as important as getting the initial business. You must stay in contact with your customer. They trusted you enough to give you the business. Now show them why they made the right choice! Follow up with your office, make sure orders have been placed, make sure manpower is set, make sure the customer still sees you're around and continue to deliver.

Any seasoned sales professional will tell you that it isn't the sale. It's the deliverable, execution, and completion of it that makes the relationship. One project at a time builds that trust and confidence in you and your organization. It is by no way easy if you're doing it right! But it will feed you for a lifetime and make you very successful over time.

YOUR PROJECT MANAGER,
YOUR "BEST FRIEND"

THIS PERSON IS so important to your success. I wanted to make a chapter just around that relationship. You know that selling externally with customers is just as important as selling internally. But the project manager will make you money or spend literally what's already in your pocket, and this is how that typical relationship flows:

1. Sales gets the order for that product/service.
2. Fulfillment team meets with sales to review the project one final time (turnover meeting).
3. Approvals are provided by leadership, and the project flows over to the fulfillment team.
4. Fulfillment leaders decide who will manage the project based on revenue, time line, and complexity.
5. Materials are ordered. Project manager (PM) hires any subcontractors and meets with the customer.
6. Time lines are confirmed, materials arrive, and the project is underway.
7. Time line is complied with, closeout items are handled, and final payments are made.

Of course, this is simplified, but this is usually how it goes for a PM. You want the PM set for success in every way. The way it worked best for me was to take that person out for a lunch once the

PM is assigned. Of course, you're buying! Discuss the project initially, possible roadblocks, key people within that organization, the time line requirements, and those deliverables. Make sure they "buy into" the project. When someone is a good PM, they truly own that project and have pride in making it profitable for all involved. They were told all this information usually during the turnover meeting, but it's always good to clear up any additional questions now. You're also trying to bond to a certain extent with your PM. Like I say, always selling.

Materials and components are ordered. Payments are tracked. The PM is dealing with subcontractors where needed, checking their work, managing the time line, and keeping everyone efficient. The PM is also holding weekly or biweekly meetings with the customer and internally. With the customer, they're talking about progress, deliverables, and completion to the time line that was agreed upon initially before it began. Internally, they're talking about those same things but also discussing the financial aspect. Because the PM must make the project profitable, it is essential that projects are performed as expected, as promised, on budget, on time line, and profitable. Did I say profitable? Maybe I should say it again!

The PM is usually tasked with "extras," meaning, they get a bonus on extra work uncovered on an existing project. They essentially are another salesperson within reason, of course. Sometimes, sales will share in that extra revenue/commission associated with that extra work found.

Two examples:

1. A medical equipment sales executive works with a local hospital on new scanning or operating equipment. Just so you're aware, some of that equipment can be seven figures! The PM is working on getting all that equipment ordered, installed, and commissioned. While at the local hospital checking on progress, the PM finds another wing of the hospital that has aged equipment.

They then talk with the local hospital's operational team, engages the sales professional, and they deliver a proposal to upgrade that other equipment, which sells!

2. A PM is working on a commercial painting project in a strip mall. While on-site, the PM walks to every store and speaks with the store owners about offering painting services while all manpower and materials are already here. Some discounts are provided to those new customers which they accept. Additional work is provided to those painters, and the PM increases revenue!

A good PM can make several thousand dollars in additional income annually if they're proficient at what they do—never charging for something that isn't beneficial to the customer! Sometimes, a PM is not compensated for additional work discovered. Then that PM is doing what is contracted most times and moving on. I'm not saying that a PM is only in it for the money, but it's human nature. If there is incentive, there is motivation!

Here is how the PM, unfortunately, can make your day real bad real fast! Let's just say the PM is potentially not really well versed in the financials. By having this deficiency, they erode a project unknowingly. For example, a subcontractor is on the project and has not managed its portion of the project well. They have significant overages on labor, and now they mention to your PM that they need additional labor and bill the project. Well, the PM then simply approves that change. It was never part of the project to give that subcontractor additional labor! That cost hits your project and erodes the profit margin. Well, now that profit has been reduced, which takes money out of your commission. That is how easily this can happen.

Or a PM is not watching a project, for example, to install custom conveyors, robotics, and machinery for XYZ Company which makes custom-made "widgets" that get delivered all over the country. So now the project time line is lost. The customer can't make this "widget" because you have gone over on your installation time line.

Well, hidden deep within the terms and conditions, it was noted by the customer, and your legal team agreed to a statement that may be worded like this: *"Loss of use due to the deficiency of an outside vendor or contractor will accompany a penalty of $50,000 per week for every week that XYZ Company can't be in production due to lack of completion of any project."*

Well, guess where that $50,000 penalty is coming from most times, the overall revenue of the project. So now that cost is directly billed against your project which is directly tied to your commission. Again, a poor PM will cost you money in the long run, and it's vital that this person succeed! You need to work closely with them, provide assistance, setting them up for success, happy customers, and profit!

THE SIMPLE STRATEGY OF INTEGRITY + DEPENDABILITY + OWNERSHIP = SPONSORSHIP

THIS CHAPTER REALLY comes down to how you have been raised or in some cases, how you have raised yourself.

Integrity means being true to your principles or in other words, honesty, having strong moral character, and being truthful.

Having integrity in sales means you need to be true to your words. What does that really mean? When you have a meeting and you're tasked with reporting back to that customer, do it. When you have a deadline that is mutually agreed upon, meet it. When you say you will do something, you better do it. That is being true to your word. That's having integrity, but don't just do it as I mention. Do your best to exceed those expectations. Show that customer you're a solid, reliable worker!

Dependability means that you're someone that can be counted on. You're there in good times and in bad to provide guidance and support.

Being dependable in sales means that you're always available to take that phone call, always there to answer that e-mail, of course, within reason. If you're in another presentation or meeting, you should not pick up another call. Don't do it! If you must take that call, please ask if you could and excuse yourself for just a minute. Keep it very brief. (The only time I would ever pick up a call is if that call is from my wife or kids.) But return that call or e-mail timely once your other meeting or appointment is over. Be there when you're needed. Show that customer they can rely on you always!

Ownership means that you're the owner or in this case, the one responsible for the relationship between company and customer, or the owner of an opportunity and driving it forward.

When you have an opportunity or a sold project, take ownership of it. Take responsibility and stay engaged. That customer looks to you when any issues arise. Don't walk away from that person or company at that moment to close other deals. Yes, you must keep selling, but be there, be present, be responsive. If you aren't, they will find someone that does as I say! Take pride in that ownership.

Sponsorship means that someone within an organization vouches for you. It means that you have proven yourself many times, and they're willing to sponsor or award you more work. Every successful and strategic sales executive has a sponsor or many sponsors, relationships!

This sponsorship doesn't happen easily. It is the end result of everything you did above. You have earned that by providing long-term guidance, support, and results. You have earned that by building that relationship!

In this scenario, the sponsorship is your payday. This person is key to your success. It's hard and can take years to earn this spot, but it's just as hard to keep that position within an organization that you sell within. Don't deviate from this strategy ever. If you do, your sponsor will question themselves and eventually go away and take their business with them!

TRUSTED BUSINESS PARTNER TO FRIEND

AS YOU SPEND years estimating, bidding, and winning proposals, the trust level within those customers/accounts you work with will increase over time. What happens is simply this. You end up making your customer's business run easier one bid at a time. This takes work away from them and gives it to you. By doing this, the customer does start to rely on you more and more. This is something that takes significant time investment and dedication on your part. It also puts more and more money into your pocket as well, which is why you do what you do!

Once you have truly gained the trust of your customer, they will ask your opinion on a project, ask for advice, even tell you what they have in their budget to do this work/project/service, etc. When someone is coming to you in that regard, they're essentially telling you they want you to direct them in the proper direction. That strategic partner is you! They want you to essentially write that RFP (request for proposal). When a customer puts you in that position, you're in the driver's seat for that project. Make sure you always have their best interest in mind. This is a coveted position. Don't screw it up!

This position of a trusted adviser is not easy to obtain, as I said. But the true sales professionals have more than one of these relationships. Some have several. That's someone we all could learn from. Look at the huge oak tree that has grown by years of hard work! Don't be jealous. Go do it for yourself. If you need insight, ask to buy that person lunch, tell them why you're buying, and pick their brain for an hour straight—time and money well spent! If that person is an eagle like you are, they will gladly help you on your way to success.

If you're a little lucky and work hard enough to become that true partner, it's a real accomplishment and something to be proud of. Usually, the relationship between sales professional and customer will grow into a friendship. This happens over several months or years spent together working on projects, conference calls, e-mails, coffee, meals, and/or social events like baseball games.

These relationships will be with a select few that become a friend. That relationship will be even harder to keep professionally since every time there's a mishap, you will get a call. This friend of yours will not want to hear any excuses also. They want things fixed and back in order; however that looks in your line of work. But that is one of the best things about sales and one of the pinnacles, making a friend. I always tell my two daughters that it isn't the number of friends. It's the quality of those select few that you earn in life. No matter what happens professionally between the two of you, remember that you have a friendship with this person, and those are to cherish.

BUILDING RELATIONSHIPS

DO YOU THINK they are important? Do you think they are a real necessity in a sales role? Please take a moment and think about it and do not read ahead.

If you said no, meaning, they really aren't that important. Well, I hate to say this, but throw this book away and go find a desk job like I mentioned in the opening!

Strong relationships are the most important thing a sales professional can have. Relationships, if they are solid, will feed you and your family for a lifetime. For example, you get a call from someone in an unrelated business, and they heard there's a project bidding in your line of work. They have the contact information of the person collecting bids, and they thought of you—relationship! A friend calls and tells you that a new building is being built, and you're an electrician/carpenter/plumber/mason, etc., and you get to submit a bid—relationship! You get a call from an old customer that moved into a new role at a company you have been trying to call on for years but had no luck—relationship!

The examples can go on and on regarding a relationship. They will either make or break you in sales. How do we build a relationship with someone? Well, it doesn't happen instantly and must grow organically. You can't push them. They grow over time. How did you get to marry your husband or wife? You didn't meet and say, "Let's go get married." You meet, you get to know one another, you have several dates, and things progress from there.

We build that relationship by the initial meeting, finding some common talking points like marriage, kids, sports teams, etc. You slowly start to build on those common themes that you share with your customer, helping them run their business in the way you know how to. If it's supplying drugs to a doctor, computer software support, insurance, office supplies, etc., it's all happening one transaction at a time. Not only are you getting to know that customer, but also you're making money and making a name for yourself.

I would always remember my old Italian father saying, "Don't tarnish our family name." Here is what this means, as you work with these people, how do you want them to talk about you? Of course, you want them to say, "He/she always stops over and says hello," "They always call and check in," "They're always picking up their phone when I call, day or night," "They always follow up when they say they will." Not only is that building your name with that customer, but it's also building your relationship, integrity, and character.

The real reward is when you hear from people in other circles, and they tell you what those other customers or people say about you. It will be positive if you're doing it right. That type of behavior will naturally breed success. Of course, if the relationship is solid, they will tease you. They will pick on you since they like you. Embrace that and laugh along at yourself! That will bring positive people into your life and additional opportunities. It's only natural since people always want to do business with people they like—relationships!

As these grow over time and if they're grown properly, your job will become easier and harder at the same time. Here's why, those customers will, of course, try to help you win work. They will speak with you about upcoming projects/bids and ask for your insight. You will help customize solutions with your company offerings. In essence, you're strategically helping drive business as a future visionary planning partner, great spot to be in, and you have earned it— strong relationship. And you should be proud.

Here is how it works against you. Now those opportunities and additional projects that you have been given are more work for you—more follow-up, more issues, additional production delays, etc. So this is a hassle and definitely more "busy work" or nonproductive selling time that needs to be spent. However, it's a necessary evil. Please don't look at it as an inconvenience. It's driven by sales, and those sales are driven from the relationship that you have. That relationship is based on years of hard work that you built! I hope that makes sense! Covet that relationship. It's much harder to build a new one than to protect a proven relationship that has been built over time. Quite simply, relationships will make you money, provide you with a comfortable life, and do so for an entire career. Protect them and keep them close always!

KNOW THE COMPETITION

EVERY INDUSTRY, OF course, has competition for what you make, offer, build, etc. But do you know who those people and companies are? Do you know how they go to market? Do you know what their strategy to grow is? Do you know if they have a competitive edge over your company? An edge over your product? If you don't, well, you better learn. I'm not saying send a covert spy employee into their organization as a new employee to gather intelligence. But are there any trusted customers or industry partners that you can go to and ask some questions? Have you researched the competitor websites? Competitors must know other competitors. It's only going to make you stronger as a sales professional.

When a team is getting ready to play against another, do they know of each other? Do they know in a sport like baseball which player they can or should not throw a fastball right over the plate to? You bet they do! In a sport like football, does one team know what players they must stop in order to gain a competitive advantage over? You bet they do so on and so on.

So you need to know which companies are bidding against you in order to gain an advantage, just like in sports. You need to know who the key sales professionals are in those companies and what their style is to a certain extent. Are they very good at bonding and rapport? Are they notorious for giving work away at almost zero profit margin? Does this other company buy projects at a loss and make it up over years of service? Again, you need to know who is trying to take the work you want. That will help you customize your approach around the bid you will submit. If you know they're notorious for bidding work at almost zero profit, make sure you talk about the extensive value in your company—how well you execute, how well you service customers in the future, and how you're very familiar with the product/service you offer. And that's why there is a cost for hiring your company. Make sure the value message is driven hard in this case. If there is one thing I've learned, it is "you get what you pay for."

Anything of value has a price in one way or another. Make sure this potential customer is well aware that good products or services come at a price. It's your job to make sure that if your bid is 10 percent, 20 percent, 30 percent, or higher than the competitors, your value message is delivered properly, and the scope of that bid is exact compared to others. Make sure other companies are bidding that same project without any deviations. That must be fully transparent. Make sure you know how the competition will approach any project, so you're leveling the playing field and making it as evenly matched as possible.

CONCEPT, IMPLEMENTATION, OPERATION, AND CONCEPT REPEATED

THAT IS A mouthful of a chapter title, isn't it? What this means is a complete lifecycle of an opportunity. When there's an internal customer team of people conceptualizing on what they want to do, they usually collaborate and come up with ideas on what to manufacture or what service they plan on offering. Well, many companies can provide services that will help a company get where they want to go. If you're involved with the initial concept and help design your solution for the customer, you're driving that opportunity. If you're doing things the right way, the business is yours.

Help develop ideas around your offerings as a sales professional in your field. Provide insight and suggest what your company can offer. But be careful with this! Don't just throw out in conversation phrases like "We can provide X" or "Our company specializes in X." Your customer knows what you do. That's why you are involved in the initial concept from the start. Or that's why you have a seat at the table! Provide insight on what your industry is offering. Speak about where the industry is moving toward, what new innovative ideas are being rolled into that market. Provide suggestions with other team members on what you have done in the past. Help steer them toward what makes sense for their organization. Be the visionary for this potential project. If you do this, they will tailor a solution in a way that your offerings will win the business!

Once the design is completed and the project bid and won by your firm ideally, now your team needs to implement the design. Sometimes, this is harder than coming up with the solution. The biggest reason why I say this is your fulfillment team. Yes, they're on your side, of course. But many times, the implementation/operations people are very task-based. They're not the visionary like the sales executive. On occasion, they will come up with more reasons why they can't do the project instead of working alongside you and finding a solution to execute the concept. This isn't a bad thing. It's simply the age-old battle between acquisition (sales) and fulfillment (operations, installation, or service teams).

When these teams get together to discuss a project that was just awarded to your company, they, many times, will not be thankful that your sale will continue to pay for their salaries, rent for the building your fellow employees occupy, health benefits, advertising, bonuses, etc. I don't mean for this to be negative. What I mean is sometimes, they don't realize this new business you just secured is job security for everyone.

Many times the fulfillment teams are also overworked, underpaid, have many projects or services to complete while being short on manpower. So as a sales professional, if you look at it from their perspective, you can understand some of the frustration. They see you sell this project, provide documentation, complete a turnover meeting, and make nice paydays! But you should help with equipment delivery delays, manufacturing delays, execution issues on the project, etc. You want to shield the customer from as much of that "noise" as you can. You need to be the tennis ball as your office and customer come at you from every angle while you bounce back and forth across the court. Stressful and annoying, yes, but who said it would be easy!

Just remember the fulfillment team has a rough job. They're in the office many more hours than you are. They're dealing with more issues than you are since there are usually several sales professionals working for a typical company. They see you come and go as you please with your fancy lunches and ball games! Many times, they will make jokes when you do decide to show up to the office, jokes like

"Look what the cat dragged in" or "Did you get lost...you came to the office." It is what it is, and in this type of role, just laugh it off. Don't feed into it, which will only fuel them more.

It's also very important that you're still out networking, taking another key customer to lunch or dinner, holding golf outings, ball games, managing your pipeline, etc. You need to backfill a pipeline while managing what is currently underway.

But getting back to your fulfillment team, remember this, you need them just as much as you need good customers and a strong pipeline of opportunities. Treat these teams with respect always. Make sure you help them and provide assistance when asked. Their success on this project will allow you to sell the next one! Don't hit and run! That will be like swinging for the fences. You will hit a few, and then fulfillment will be done with you! You can bring in all the business possible, but if there's no one there to execute and support you, it's over! You must build relationships with your fulfillment teams just as well like any customer.

Once all is sold, designed, implemented, and operational, now you can start looking into the next concept. Keep your mind on the task. Help with all aspects of "cradle to grave and back to cradle." Simply put, design it, install it, operate it until it's at the end of its useful life, and design it again. You got this!

SALES "TALK"

HOW DO SALESPEOPLE speak? Well, they sometimes talk with terms that may seem foreign. Here, I will discuss some of the most popular terms so there's a better understanding of what they mean. Sales pros, you can skip this section ☺.

Volume: Simple one—it just means how much was sold. If a sales rookie sold $100,000 in new business, the "volume" is $100,000. This may also be called "revenue."

Gross profit: If the volume above is $100,000 and there's a 20 percent "gross profit," that's $20,000 in profit earned for the seller and company.

Margin expansion: This is what the strong sales professionals always strive toward. For example, what I mentioned above in having 20 percent gross profit. Well, this seller can expand that to maybe 25 or 30 percent. This is done by holding precise turnover meetings, expediting shipping or the deliverable. It can also be done by utilizing the right labor for the sale and staying involved like a project manager. When a seller drives "margin expansion," it's money in the bank! There's usually a financial reward for the seller here.

Margin erosion: This is what happens when the above *margin expansion* is not executed, and maybe it wasn't sold properly. If the time line is not followed, materials were accidentally omitted from the bid, the labor pool utilized does not match the sale. When we don't worry about the deliverable and time line, then that costs money. You will not go back to the customer for additional funds. This is "margin erosion." Then many sellers that have a compensation plan that matches margin will, of course, earn less. No fulfillment team, sales professional, or sales manager wants erosion of a profit margin. Usually, everyone is ranked in this specific area.

Executed profit: If that same example is utilized, that gross profit was $20,000 or 20 percent. In this example, the materials and/or equipment was ordered timely, the turnover meetings were clear, everyone knew their role in the process, the deliverable was made on time, and the project was a complete success. So all those things delivered an increased "executed profit" to let's say 24 or 26 percent. Job well done, and the boss will be happy with you!

Recurring revenue: This is the volume that comes into your organization automatically with zero or very minimal effort. As a consumer, you might pay the phone company $100 per month for your monthly phone and data usage. Well, that phone company has "recurring revenue" from you for a total of $100 per month.

Change order: Let's say you hire a local contractor to build an addition to your home that costs $150,000. While working on that addition, he notices your kitchen cabinets are antiques and are hardly being held up by the rusted old door hinges. He discusses with you the possibility of installing all-new cabinets, flooring, and whatever else needed. So to do this work, there is a "change order" to the existing volume of $150,000 for an additional $50,000. Well, that change order is worth $50,000 to the initial project, making the total project value now $200,000. So it's simply additional revenue sold above and beyond an initial sale.

Value proposition: Why you? Why your company? What is your message? What makes you so special? That is the "value proposition" and the reason why the customer will lose if they don't pick you! The value message is in your proposal and have those reasons identified. You must discuss them during the presentation phase and the "why" they need you, and the reason why not choosing your company would have a negative impact.

ROI: Return on investment can be challenging to execute. You must justify your work with financial analysis which must be outlined in your proposal to the customer. The presentation will be precise, outlining future savings of a product or service. So if they approve the XYZ project, the savings will be so significant that it will pay for the initial sale in one year, two years, etc.

Quick example: You're a sales professional that sells high-efficient solar panels that generate electricity. If XYZ building buys this solar application, their electricity bills would be reduced by thousands monthly. You have a meeting with the building owner to discuss all the wonderful features and benefits of these solar panels. What that building owner, facilities manager, or CFO wants to know is, What is the "return on investment?" So if they pay you for the electrical modifications and solar arrangements, how long will it take to pay back the initial cost? After that period, then the benefit is truly provided to that customer for future savings. If the time line for that "ROI" is somewhat short, meaning, one to three years, your value proposition is clear. You should have earned yourself a sale!

Profit and loss (P&L): This is how someone tracks all company expenses like salaries, rent, health benefits, phone, IT and computer fees, utilities, travel expenses, advertising, and truly any expense it takes to run a business. I'm going into this simply so you're aware that most companies have someone running and analyzing all expenses within an organization by software or spreadsheet. So if and when someone speaks of the "P&L" statement, you understand, and it's typically an accountant or financial officer within an organization. If there's significant travel in your role like in mine, the financial officer may complain about your monthly expense report for airfare, hotel, rental cars, customer meals, and other business entertainment. When they do, make sure you use that travel expense as a justification for the large sale you helped close. Make sure it's all documented to justify the expense outlined since travel costs can stick out as some of the highest costs within an organization. The P&L of a company is the true indicator of the company and its health—how every aspect is tracked and where the excess in a company will be found and trimmed and the profitable segments elaborated upon.

C-suite: This means "chief suite" is where the chief executive, chief financial, chief technology, and other chief level officers reside. This is the place where any sales professional is trying to make progress in building relationships. When you have a relationship formed at levels such as these, the job can become quite easy!

OPPORTUNITIES

WE ARE DRIVEN people and confident in ourselves as sales professionals. We know there will be many ups and downs in business. We need to understand that and ride the ebb and flow of the business cycle. But we also need to create opportunities for ourselves, thinking strategically, working on long-term goals and objectives with our customers.

We don't need to, as I say, push a button or pull a lever like a desk job doing the same thing over and over, year after year, or work in manufacturing, producing the same widget day in and day out. There is nothing wrong with those types of jobs, but sales is very different. It is always moving, changing, and throwing you a curveball as they say. But the key is to find the opportunity to drive sales business! Getting that "yes" is the goal!

For example, a price is needed for a product and/or service. The customer says it is due today, so rush and get it completed. What they really should be saying is that they forgot about an upcoming project, and now they are at the end of the deadline. So, of course, their lack of planning is your fire drill. Get used to it. It is sales! When you comply and do as requested, they will trust you, and the credibility is growing. This exercise should be the exception and not the standard with that customer.

Then they want your proposal revised to add products and/or services. A decision is to be made by the customer this week, yeah! We will win the work for sure, you say. Then a week, a month, a year goes by, no answer, and the customer has gone MIA (missing in action). But then surprisingly, your phone rings, or you get that e-mail. They want to revisit all that again, going through the same processes time and time again. And as always, the customer goes MIA! I have seen that transpire plenty of times. This time, you might just win! Yes, of course, you will win for sure this time. We have done this exercise three or four times. But that doesn't happen. The project is delayed, or those funds are used elsewhere. When it pops up year after year, run! Tell them to put 5 percent on top of your proposal from last year. Update the date on your proposal and spend no more than five minutes on it! Losing that opportunity will be an addition by subtraction for those customers.

Now listen, really listen here. If this is happening in one of your select or key accounts, you are to blame! You should be assisting and driving that opportunity. Where is your strategic vision for that customer? Where is your planning for the future? You are basically no different than any other vendor that sells what you do! Change that mindset. Set yourself apart from the competition! Now if this is happening with someone literally calling you off the street, just spend your time elsewhere where it is much more useful. Your time is so very valuable, and where you choose to spend it directly relates to dollars in or out of your pocket!

Opportunities like those you don't need. Any procurement or purchasing person (that is someone that usually acquires bids and delegates who will be awarded the work) will play this with you over and over. Honestly, many could care less if they ever give you the work! They just need updated pricing, and they need to send your bid back into their boss just in case the project, service, or product is approved. But what if your tree had roots in the purchasing or procurement departments? If you do, then you usually avoid this evil cycle of bid and rebid. Again, a sales professional thinking strategically with a vision of the future with this customer is helping drive the opportunity, so it truly never goes to a bid situation if you can avoid it. You're helping them with their job and also helping push business in your direction completely normal and very tactical. Down and deep those roots go (your strategic position) and strengthen into the earth (being your customer's organization).

Another example is the customer calls you and says, "I have $100,000 in my budget this year for your widget/service [fill in as needed]. How quickly can you get me the proposal?" You will have plenty of those calls and e-mails if you stay in sales for a career. Crazy, right? But it's true! Companies usually get money to spend for their calendar or fiscal year. Sometimes, that money just doesn't get used. So in order for them to get that money back next year through a budget, it must be spent! So luckily, that call, that person they thought of, that relationship you're building or have built comes to you! They like you, enjoy your company, feel they need to do something for your company since what you offer is something they always want and need. Why do they feel this way? Because you're the sales executive, you've invested time, understand their company, their culture, key people, the vision they strive for, learn about them personally as well over coffee, lunches, outside the office events, etc.

Any type of sales job has its own reasons to find opportunities to drive sales—from a front desk clerk at a gym signing you up for extra classes to your local lawn care company pushing extra chemical or bug control treatments. Possibly, it's your insurance agent calling and asking you to increase coverage or to buy an additional enhanced plan. Your car mechanic is telling you to do that extra "just in case" repair. They're all opportunities for those people to win business, big or small dollars. Many times, these people just fall in line with the masses of sellers. Be better than that, prove your worth, be a cut-above strategic thinker!

But to become a true professional, you need to be able to withstand the low periods, uncover opportunities, discard opportunities that are simply not valid, determine if a project is a "go or no go," as they say. This simply means, yes, we will bid, or no, we won't since we determine it isn't valid. When valid, customize a true solution to benefit the customer. Then once it's sold and you have gotten the "yes," execute well, provide a profitable sale for your company, and make money for yourself!

Immediate opportunities, emergency projects, repeat or long-term, all are reasons to drive revenue/sales. But worst of all, the no-chance opportunity when you're continually called for pricing and a solution and none are ever sold. Fire them! Yes, you can actually fire a customer with good reason, as I mentioned. If there truly is no relationship to build because the customer will never see you, doesn't value what your company offers, or doesn't want to deal with you, but they have to, all along you know they have no intention of giving you the business, move on!

Make sure management is in agreement with you. Time is money as they say. If they have all the details and examples from you regarding that company, most likely, they will fire them for you by telling them to take your company off their list of providers or vendors. You don't have to pursue every opportunity that comes across your path. Now if your boss is telling you to do so, then you must. But a true sales leader will stand behind the team and help them sell. Most managers are paid a bonus off your hard work anyway, so it's in their best interest to help you succeed (I will talk about management in a later chapter).

Profit Margin Is Not Markup

Profit margin or gross profit is the sale of an item minus COGS (cost of goods sold). Those costs can be related to what it takes to build your product and those labor expenses. Simply put, any expense directly related to those products intended to be sold are part of COGS. These are outlined on income statements which make true profit easier to identify.

Definition of profit margin or gross profit is defined as net sales minus COGS.

Margin example:
If someone sells a widget for $10, and costs $8 to build, the gross profit or gross margin is $2. The gross margin is 20% (2 divided by 10 which is .20 or 20%).

Markup example:
That widget still costs $8 and sells at $10 again. The markup is $2 (same as gross profit). However, the markup is a percentage of the product cost (not sale price). The $2 markup is divided by the cost of $8 and the markup is 25% (2 divided by 8 which is .25 or 25%).

So with this simple example, the difference is 5% of a $10 sale. Do a few examples on your own, increase those figures and you will find those differences between margin and markup become significant. I always price to margin, never markup since markup can appear to be a false perception of higher profit.

The surprising thing in this example is many sales executives, and even some sales leaders, don't know this. It's not their fault. It's a sign of a new versus old generational selling. For as long as sales were made, someone was typing or writing out an estimate doing this example I mentioned above. In the world of computers, people simply input that into their system, ask for the desired margin, and get the answer. What happens when your network goes down? Even worse, when the network goes down and you have the biggest project of your career due, of course, that day? At least, buy yourself a sales calculator that will have that functionality already built in. This way, you can still price what is needed until your network is revived. In the next section, there is a more in-depth example of pricing a product, service, etc.

PRICING EXERCISES

. . . .

NOW THAT YOU have gotten an opportunity to bid, how do you price it? Where do we set the profit margins? Here are simple examples that can be used for any type of business by using simple math examples.

(Tip: buy that sales calculator that can price profit margins and save time)

Example #1: We are pricing how someone may buy Widget-X.

This is fairly straightforward. Let's say the product costs $1,000.

1. Product—$1,000
2. Manufacturing or expediting fees—$250
3. Delivery charges—$150
4. Warranty of the product—$150
5. This totals $1,550 of cost to your company.

So a break-even price is $1,550 (this means no profit...we don't ever want that).

Now to assign margin dollars, you usually need to speak with your sales manager in many cases depending on the value, your fulfillment team as well since they will need to execute on what you sell. You will all need to agree on what margin to price this at. This is tricky, but remember my mindset (singles and doubles since they will always allow you to get back up to bat and swing again by bidding another time for that customer). The opportunity being brought to you by phone call, e-mail, or bid invitation is the chance to get back up to the plate, to swing at the pitch!

Your estimate, internal bid meeting, the agreed pricing with margin, the proposal you type, and the presentation is the swing!

We assigned a 40 percent profit margin (could be higher or lower and the opportunity qualification will determine margin most times) that puts us at a selling price of $2,583 to purchase Widget-X.

If we wanted a 40 percent markup, it would bring us to a selling price of $2,170—big difference and a mistake many seasoned sales-people make unfortunately since that would make that profit margin much lower.

Always price to margin, not markup, in my opinion. By using the markup example, this project is selling at about 29 percent margin— much lower than the 40 percent you could have had if you priced to margin.

Example #2: We will be pricing on how to sell labor services.

Let's say the same applies to purchase Widget-X, but now we will install it. We know that our Widget-X costs $2,583 with a 40 percent profit margin.

1. Widget-X—$2,583
2. Labor hours needed for example could be two technicians for one working day on normal business hours (usually Monday to Friday from 8:00 a.m. to 4:30 p.m.), sixteen hours in total

This is when you speak to your fulfillment team, service department, or lead person and ask if they're okay with those hours. You need to have a clue as to what you're trying to sell. They will respect that. Don't just say, "How many hours do I need?" Call your field team and ask their opinion. Do your research and find out what it takes. Like I've said, learn your craft! Show that you're making an attempt to make their job a little easier! You don't have to be that technical expert, but you need a clue so when your customer calls and has a question, at least you can speak in general terms about what you're proposing.

They agree on that labor and have given you verbal or documented approval. They will execute the project with that amount of labor. *A very important step, you always need the approval of your fulfillment or service teams that will actually execute the work.*

Let's say that burden cost (burden is the cost of salary, benefits, vehicle expenses, training, and other costs that might be included in that technical installation cost) is some obscure number since they typically are due to the mathematics involved. Maybe that cost is $108 per/hr depending on what type of labor and where geographically this will be sold and installed. For this example, we will use the $108.

Now the cost is $108 per/hr (multiplied by two since it will take two people one working day on normal hours, which is usually from 7:00 a.m. or 8:00 a.m. to 3:30 p.m. or 4:30 p.m.).

Note: If this were an overtime situation, you typically would charge the normal hours rate multiplied by 1.5 for that differential of half time for the after-hours or Saturday rate. If this were the case, this rate would be $162 per/hr. If this project were to be installed on a Sunday or national holiday, it would typically be a double-time rate of $216 per/hr, but the same example applies regardless of when the work would be done.

Our labor cost is now $1,728 ($108 burden rate per/hr x 16 hours) without making any profit on the project labor. If we want to assign, let's say a 30 percent margin on our labor, the selling price of this would now be $2,469 at a 30 percent margin.

Note: A quick way to determine that is to divide the $1,728 into the $2,469, which equals to .699 minus .699 from 1 and that equals 0.301 or .30 or 30 percent profit. Another example is if I wanted to price the labor at a 50 percent margin, that cost would be $3,456 by taking the $1,728 divided by $3,456, which is .50 (again that minus 1 is a 50 percent margin).

It is important to know how to price in this manner. Now spend $20. Buy an inexpensive sales calculator that can price to margin and save a few steps and let the calculator do it for you!

So the revised example to purchase and install Widget-X looks like this:

1. Product—$2,583
2. Labor hours needed is two technicians for one working day on normal business hours—$2,469
3. Miscellaneous supplies—$75

Your bid is $5,127.

Miscellaneous supplies, trip charges, or fuel fees are things to be cautious with.

Here are a few reasons for each. Miscellaneous fees are warranted when the opportunity exists. For example, if you're a car mechanic and you need to replace an engine, there are many added costs that go with that other than the engine and labor costs. There could be oil and fluid disposal charges that a third-party vendor charges. There could be extensive charges for the old engine to be discarded at a junkyard. Removing a defective engine and installing a new one is not easy or clean, so who pays for all the incidentals needed? If you say the mechanic, no way! The customer always pays! This is not a way to overcharge or sell something not needed. This is simply a way to cover your fees that are the cost of doing business.

You're running a business to make money, not have margin erosion. That erosion is trailing costs not carried in an estimate, and when those fees do hit the bottom line, they destroy your earned profit. Margin erosion happens when you don't account for those incidental charges. For the car mechanic example, it could be rags, degreasers, cleaners, miscellaneous bolts, bracketing, or whatever "consumable" items a car mechanic would utilize. These "consumable materials" must be used, or you can't replace that engine. Those added costs or fees, if not accounted for, are what would reduce your profit margin or equate to margin erosion. *Your costs must be accounted for in every bid. A very important message again, your costs must always be accounted for in every bid.*

A good mechanic will know what those costs are and spell them out in the miscellaneous section of the invoice. So there is full transparency, and the costs are covered, maintaining the profit margin. They can be listed like degreasers/rags, $13; miscellaneous hardware/bracketing, $14; electrical wiring modifications required for a new engine, $28. Of course, these are not exact costs, but you will need to know what they are. This practice isn't insignificant because it is!

Think about this $55 I mentioned above in the car engine example:

1. If this car mechanic replaces two engines weekly with $55 in miscellaneous fees per engine
2. That yearly fee becomes $5,720 of profit margin gain
3. That would have been an erosion of margin to a total of $5,720 per year—just in that one segment of being a car mechanic
4. Instead, that is margin gain in that specific area of the car repair business

Apply that same mindset to replacing alternators, batteries, tires, brakes, oil changes, and whatever else a car mechanic does! Miscellaneous fees are a *significant* way to cover accrued costs and make a profit, not lose money without realizing it!

Mileage charges or fuel fees are also ways of covering costs and not allowing margin erosion. These fees can apply in all industries that deliver, service, install, manufacture, or any type of business that your team will need to "roll a truck" to a customer.

This fee can be applied per mile if you're tracking it that closely. This will usually be a way to completely stand behind any argument a customer may have. For example, your delivery person is coming from the warehouse, making a delivery to a home or business 150 miles away. That is a significant distance. So maybe your company charges $.50 per mile, and his GPS report can be provided to that customer to see the route he took. It must be the most direct route in order to make that delivery. In this case, a charge of $75 would apply. Again, let's see how this would break down by the end of one year:

Two deliveries daily at $75 each (remember this fee is for each delivery/service truck) multiplied by a typical five-day workweek. That is $750 for that week and a yearly total of $39,000 per vehicle ($150 per day × five days is $750 per/week × 52 weeks)! This charge per mile is a variable depending on each geographic location that you operate in. Simply put, you could not charge delivery fees in Omaha, Nebraska, what you would charge in San Francisco or New York City. But these are real fees that should be included in all bids to avoid that margin erosion!

Example #3: Product sale, install labor, including miscellaneous fees along with fuel charges

Here is the setting, ABC Corporation called a local HVAC company since their building was 85 degrees when they walked in on Monday morning. Of course, it was the "dog days" of summer, mid-August, and the high for the day was 95 degrees with high humidity, typical summer day!

The technician Rob came out and found that a thirty-year-old commercial HVAC system installed on the roof was beyond repair. Since this one massive unit heated and cooled the entire building, the replacement cost would be significant. The technician called Frank, the senior sales executive assigned to ABC Corporation. Since it would be a complex replacement and time was what they didn't have, Frank ran right out to ABC as he should, and together with Rob, they came up with a solution. During this time, everyone went home since it was just too hot to work indoors. ABC Corporation lost productive time in the office, which has also cost them money!

Luckily there was one massive unit in stock at a local distributor, and Frank would price this as follows:

Burden costs for ABC Corporation's HVAC system replacement:

1. New HVAC Unit—$38,500

2. Trucking and deliver—$350
3. Installation labor—two technicians three days each (forty-eight hours with burden cost of $98 per/hr)—$4,704
4. Administrative fees (office personnel filing for municipal permits)—$30 for office personnel's time and $250 in permit fees—$280
5. Crane fees (must contract with a local crane company to remove the old and install the new)—$5,000
6. Airflow-ductwork modifications—$4,200
7. Electrical modifications to adapt to the new unit—$3,700
8. Miscellaneous degreasers, rags, and hardware—$150
9. Disposal fee of the old system—$125
10. Fuel charge of $10 per truck/per day (another way to account for fuel and/or mileage fees)—$60

When pricing gets to this level of complexity or greater, it's best to use a spreadsheet to easily look at burden costs and sell prices, but please remember to *price for margin and not markup*.

Sell prices noted below are rounded off.

Line Number and (Burden Cost)	Margin % Add	Sell Price
#1 (38,500)	25	51,333
#2 (350)	30	500
#3 (4,704)	40	7,840
#4 (280)	15	329
#5 (5,000)	10	5,556
#6 (4,200)	20	5,250
#7 (3,700)	20	4,625
#8 (150) cover cost or add margin?	0	150
#9 (125) cover cost or add margin?	15	147
#10 (60) cover cost or add margin?	0	60
Total Burden Cost of $57,069		**$75,790**

Bid price is dividing those final "burden" costs into the selling price, which comes out to be 25 percent. Now, if you feel you have a very strong possibility of winning a project similar (regardless of what you sell solutions for) and you also know it's not to be a bid to other competitors, possibly add more margin—again, your call! Maybe go in at a 30 percent margin. That would be $57,069 divided by $81,527, and that is .70, which is a 30 percent margin—remember "singles and doubles."

Of course, the simple way is using that sales calculator and plugging in your costs and utilizing the margin button as desired. So it doesn't matter what you sell and have solutions for—medical equipment, printers, copiers, computer software, HVAC, cars, etc. Burden costs relate, profit margins relate, and so do the opportunities themselves. It's all finding that opportunity, customizing that solution, and presenting it to the customer in order to win, hearing that "yes!"

What I've always loved about a format like above is that you can adjust those margins as needed very quickly. This way, different categories can carry different margins which should help give you a competitive edge against the competition. I also ask on lines 8, 9, and 10 what *you* should do in this pricing example. There truly is no right or wrong answer. Just remember the singles and doubles I have taught you.

At this point, Frank has all his costs covered along with margins. He speaks with the sales/installation managers and gets their approval to bid that price. *He formulates his proposal and pays close attention to detail in what he writes. It is neat, in order, and has no spelling errors. He prints a few color copies and then meets with the facilities manager at ABC to win this project!* You must already see the project won in your mind before you even meet. You always know you will win, positive visualization always, visualizing hearing the "yes!"

A project priced with these margins should be competitive and have an opportunity to sell. What will differentiate you from the competition here is your deliverable. You have located what the customer needs locally and can have it done ASAP. Don't lower that margin, push the value in why they called your company, boast about your ability to perform the job, and ask for the business! You have spent the time with this customer. *You have earned the right then ask!*

The worst that can happen is when you hear a "no." It is sales. We hear that word sometimes. The key is to hear "yes" a lot more!

Just a comment, that strategic thinker senior sales executive has already met with the customer in the past about this project. It has already been budgeted for, so in this scenario, Frank would ask for the business since the research and proposal have already been provided. Strategic planning has set Frank apart from the others. The customer has already budgeted for this system replacement, and it's not done in the middle of the summer. It's done on a nice spring or fall day. There are now no interruptions in the workday or lost time in the office, subsequently saving ABC Corporation money. You see, Frank has proven himself to ABC by proposing this replacement and having the vision of what could and eventually will happen. Frank will have a very hard time losing any future business from ABC. They're with Frank for the long term. He is a business partner, a visionary, a strategic thinker, and miles apart from the competition. Nice work, Frank!

SALES GOALS

WE ALL HAVE goals to reach in one way or another. Goals are meant to be achieved. If you're a customer service agent at a car repair center, most likely you're tracked by how many additional services you suggest and sell. If you're working the counter at a fast-food restaurant, you're gauged by how many additional items you can sell in addition to what the customer is asking for. If you're a local HVAC contractor working in homes day after day, you're usually assigned a sales target on Wi-Fi thermostats, upgraded safeties, better filtration, etc. to help your central air or heating system operate more efficiently and improve air quality. My point with these examples is, we all have goals to achieve.

In a sales role, goals are the driver above all else. If you're a top performer year after year and you exceed goals without much effort, maybe they're set too low. If you're giving it your best year after year and the goals are never attained, maybe they're set too high. Perhaps the account base between that high performer and the underachiever needs to be reset. Maybe some of those accounts assigned to you will always be plentiful, and others will always be stagnant. Those variables should be looked at by leadership and assigned properly between sales professionals. Or the worst, *you just aren't that good and should consider a different role within your company. It's okay. Not everyone can do this!*

That is where a sales leader/manager must understand the market business and where to set those goals. They want you to win! They want you to succeed since any sales manager I've worked for always received a bonus if their team exceeded the goals or targets. Is it important that the goals of the company are realistic for the organization? For example, corporate assigns growth goals of 30 percent on all offices and all its sales professionals. They also demand that all projects are sold at a 40 percent profit margin! Here is the issue with this scenario. Not only are the growth goals set where they are but also the profit margin is set very high as well. Did corporate look at trends in your market? Did they analyze the data to determine if these goals are realistic?

If you work for a large corporation sometimes at the top, they drive people toward goals that are simply not attainable, and they know it! They really wanted 20 percent growth but will overdrive their teams to get desired results. Sounds like a shell game, doesn't it? Many times, when a CEO drives teams to this level and those goals are actually reached, bonuses can be in the millions for that CEO-type person!

If you work for a smaller local company, usually, the sales manager partners with the president to strategize on what the upcoming yearly sales goals should be. They look at the data and, of course, have a "wish list" goal, but they will not overdrive the sales team to get there. They value those employees and know how important they are to the company and its future success. In a large organization, many times, they simply fire lower-level sales talent and continue to hire new until that killer sales executive is found.

When you're giving it your all, accounts have been realigned, you have guidance from leadership, and things still aren't hitting, you need to stay the course! Show your leadership how hard you're working to drive business. If you get their buy-in and work closely with your manager, you should be okay and not in jeopardy of losing your job! However, if this doesn't improve within a year or two, you may be looking for a job regardless. Like I mentioned earlier, you have to be strong, determined, and confident since goals and actual sales don't lie. The proof is in the results!

Don't complain and be the person that says your quota is not fair. Don't provide five reasons as to why you can't make your goals. Positive thinking and a strong outlook toward the future always like

I said earlier. Remember the chickens and eagles! Negative talk just brings the negative to reality. Negative thoughts make those negative things become a reality. Positive thoughts and conversations with a strong outlook for the future will drive that winning culture.

If you're exceeding your goals, good for you! This means that in theory, you're doing everything correctly. Now you can spend more time on conceptualizing a new project or service. Since your overall numbers are in excess of the targets, it will allow you to drive more future business. Plant those seeds and grow that tree for the future! This will sustain your sales and keep you on top!

Here is a little secret, if you're overdriving your targets and coming into the close of the year, great! But *keep a project or two aside and let the year close out* for that calendar or fiscal year. As a professional, you know they will be adding, at a minimum, 10 percent on top of what you already brought in this past year. Keep that revenue aside as long as you can. Ideally, you keep it until the new goals are set, then *whamo*! You just added a project to your new year, one that was in your back pocket! Any sales leader frowns on this behavior. But any good sales leader was a sales professional at one point in their career, and they get it. They understand and did the same! Of course, the customer must be okay with this. And with *a strong customer relationship*, you can ask this favor of them.

A friend of mine, John, who has been in a sales role for a good twenty years, is famous for this. This guy keeps high six-figure projects off the books until the new fiscal year. Never fails, once the new fiscal year is active, it goes for booking, and he starts off the year with a project that takes most people two months to accumulate! Good ole Johnny boy, what a nice guy personally as well! This is not unethical behavior. It's being strategic with your assigned sales target versus your actual performance. You should always be working the numbers and driving results!

RESULTS VERSUS PIPELINE

RESULTS ARE EASY to see. They're in your company database, printed out, and spoken of during sales meetings among the sales team. Or they're simply on a whiteboard in the break room. All that shows is how hard you've been working and driving results. If you're working hard but still not on top of the pack, you will be. It's simply taking longer, and that seed needs constant water! Those results will be there at some point soon enough. But why do sales leaders do this? No one wants to be at the bottom. It does drive sales behavior and results. Sales leaders know this and always encourage healthy sales interaction and competition.

But the pipeline is tricky. Are those potential sales that you fore-casted true? Do you know if those projects will ever sell? Or do you carry them from year to year in hopes they will at some point sell? If the last one is what you're hoping for, remove it from the pipeline. That sales pipeline is truly what you predict to generate in sales volume. If you continue to input projects in "hopes" they will sell, well, you may as well "hope" to hit the lottery. It's not a real opportunity and focus on what is reality.

Your pipeline must have a true opportunity investigated by you and/or your team collectively. What are they trying to accomplish? Have you customized this solution alongside them? Are you viewed as a vendor or a true business partner? Do they want you to win? Or do they just need a "number" from you? Once those are determined, you need to have a verbal conversation with your customer. Explain to them that you will be putting this into your sales pipeline. Let them know that you will be following up on that agreed-upon date/season. You will be asking for the business. You did the research, presentation, and follow-up activities. You have earned the right to ask for the business! Too many times, we just don't simply ask for the business. You must! But realistically, do you think this opportunity will sell? What is your vision telling you? Listen to this in order to be precise in your forecast and pipeline.

A pipeline is not something sales professionals/executives do to appease their manager. Yes, the manager also forecasts future business from it. But it's your gauge on how bright or dim your sales future is. Make it true, make it real, and make it shine brightly! If you don't do this and you're someone that doesn't maintain the pipeline, I can say this with confidence, your sales manager will be speaking to you about your forecast and vision of future sales. Remember, your boss was most likely a sales executive at one time. Don't try to "sell" them on your forecast. They will then turn it around, push down on you harder, and make things more difficult. The good ones won't even tell you they could smell you and your half-baked pipeline coming a mile away—not a good position to be in with the boss.

Be honest and work the pipeline as you should. Make it a living thing that you maintain regularly. It will guide you toward your goals and make sure to utilize it as a constant reminder of what you're committing to. A good sales manager, knowing you're honest and diligent, will see where you need help and will try to maneuver opportunities around where you could use that help—backfilling that pipeline, providing more opportunities for sales success, and driving results!

WHAT'S YOUR PLAN TO MAKE YOUR PLAN (P2MP)?

WHEN HAVING A sales quota assigned to you, the expectation is, of course, that you will attain and hopefully exceed it. Where did this quota come from? Are you ready to speak about the plan and how you will accomplish it? How do you prepare for the P2MP?

The quota is assigned by the sales manager and is based on what's in the pipeline of new business you are forecasting compared to company goals. If you have three opportunities in your pipeline for one million dollars each, will you sell all three? I'm a positive thinking person, but realistically, the answer is no. You need three opportunities to close one, and you also want triple in pipeline compared to the annual goal. The sales manager will most likely assign that million-dollar number or more as a starting point. In addition, there is usually a stretch goal of a certain percentage added to the annual goal. A good manager will know how much to add and how much they can challenge you to achieve goals.

In addition to the pipeline and stretch goal, historical analysis is usually completed. What has that customer purchased from your company? For example, over the last three years, they purchased $500,000 in year 1, $350,000 in year 2, and $650,000 in year 3. How do you gauge that future pipeline and utilize it in a forecast or for your P2MP? Well, that annual average is $500,000. Add all three years and divide it by three, which is a simple way to have an accurate estimate. My point here is that you could have a P2MP meeting based on this data monthly, quarterly, or annually; but goodness I hope it isn't monthly! Educate yourself and understand this information so you're more than ready.

A P2MP happens for many reasons, and you must be prepared. It is a way for a sales manager to see what you have been doing and what you're working on. It's also a great way for you to truly look at the pipeline to see where there are shortfalls and overages. Then, adjust effort accordingly based on that pipeline and booked sales compared to annual goals. A sales manager does want you to make quota to keep you happy, financially secure, motivated, and employed. It's up to you, however, to really understand the assigned accounts, how they buy, what they buy, and when they buy.

Quick side note: *Understand your compensation plan since there is always one constant,* it will change. *Sales compensation plans are always under scrutiny because sales executives are usually some of the highest earners within an organization. It will be adjusted to incentivize sellers for results in areas where the company needs growth the most. Know your plan to help the company and maximize your personal income potential.*

Now back to your P2MP. Most of these meetings will include your immediate supervisor, usually the manager this person reports to, and many times top executive(s) within the organization. These people attend because the P2MP is vital to the success of the company. The goals of the overall organization are usually in direct relation to you and your sales team. The reality in any business is that sales are what keeps the company in business! Do you think the executives want to be part of these meetings? Of course, they do!

In many P2MPs, you're provided a template so everyone has the same documents or slides for data entry. Make sure you have the proper organizational chart of your customer's leadership, local or national (whatever applies to your sales role). You also need to have touch points with these people. If you don't, make sure you have them before your P2MP meeting.

Inspect your customer's website and educate yourself on how many employees they have, what their annual revenue is, and what product or service they specialize in. In addition to those details, read over the Environmental, Social, and Governance (ESG) Report if they have one. That will outline how a company communicates its initiatives toward the environment (battling climate change, reducing its greenhouse gas emissions, renewable energy, waste reduction, and so forth), social (how the company nurtures its workforce, labor practices, health and safety, and so forth), and governance (policies and procedures, executive leadership compensation disclosure, business ethics, and so forth). Read their mission statement, and does it align with yours? Where is there overlap, and how can you adapt your selling strategy for future success?

When it comes time for your P2MP, make sure you have practiced the presentation a few times verbalizing it alone or in front of someone. You don't read the entire P2MP, but be familiar with the data and be mindful of the "umm and ahh." Silence between sections is much better than filling the dead air with brutal words like those.

Present to this team like you would any customer. Clearly outline the data in an overview, but like I said, don't talk to each sentence or bullet point on a slide. Let the team read the data, and you speak of the relationship you're building, the solid pipeline, or sold book of business. You can also speak of your strategy to expand within this account. In addition, talk about how your unique offerings will continue to grow sales along with the relationship you're building stronger with the customer.

Be prepared for probing questions, and this will be the standard for most of these meetings. Leadership will want to understand this account and how well you know them. Think of it as an interrogation in a way. Do not take offense to their critiquing and constant questions. Start your answer with something like, "Great question," or "Glad that you asked." Don't make that an annoying way to start every answer but learn your style, and it will flow easily over time. Management will see that you're open to positive criticism, which shows signs of professional maturity. A P2MP is around your top five to ten accounts. The meetings are set for about an hour or so and go over schedule regularly due to collaboration. So be ready with your material, practice, relax, and execute. Keep the good attitude, laugh, and have some fun!

Once completed, make sure you thank the team for their time. But go a step further, also thank them for their efforts around helping you succeed because some sellers may think these meetings are a way for management to get on you about what you're not doing or where you could do better. Don't look at it that way. Think of it as a meeting with leadership that's fully committed to making you as successful as they possibly can. When you win, so does the company!

SALES CHARTS/GRAPHS

REPORTING OF PROGRESS within a sales group is a necessity. If you're at the bottom, you will hate this chart. If you're the top performer, of course, this will be your favorite part of your day—having that team meeting with the sales leader will be a complete joy. Charts are a must, but complexity is not! Many times, the sales manager wants to show how savvy they are with reports and charts. Just stop. It's not needed. Keep it as simple as possible so you can focus on overall volume compared to assigned goals and then, of course, the gross profit component. Take a moment and look at sales executive #1, #2, and #3. You also have our new junior sales associate. Look and decide who is the most profitable for this company. Pretty easy to read, not an eyesore with arrows, percentages or past years performance comparisons. Sure, you do need to compare YOY (year-over-year, meaning from one year to the next) growth or deficiency, but that's what the sales leader should do in a one-on-one meeting alone with you, not in a group setting ever.

This bar chart is for overall team performance, bragging rights for the leader, and a simple way for your team to see results, reward, and outline deficiencies. This is *all* you need to gauge a sales team. The only other piece that can be helpful is executed profit. That's directly tied to the fulfillment team, which can vary for several reasons (remember the project manager chapter).

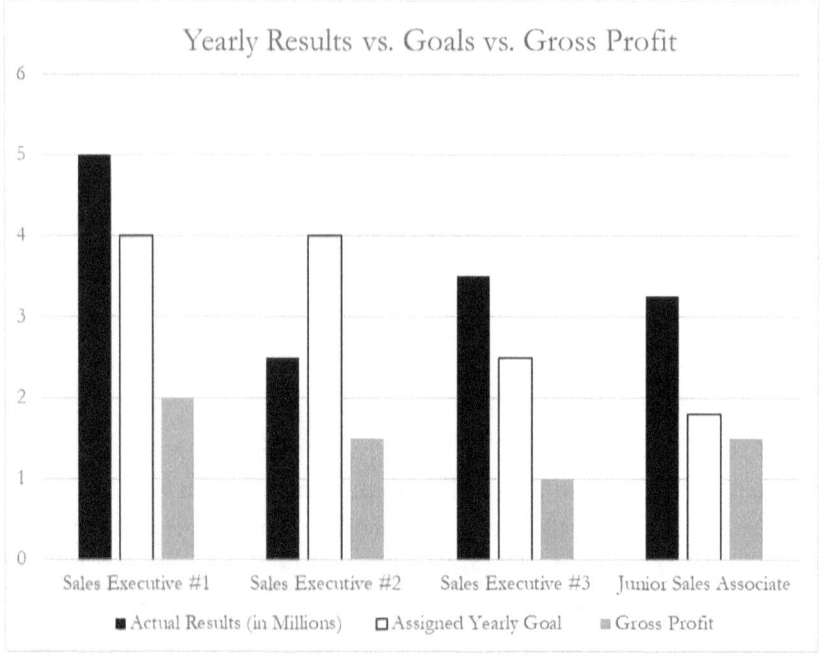

Sales executive #1: *Actual volume $5M assigned yearly goal $4M gross profit $2M*

Sales executive #2: *Actual volume $2.5M assigned yearly goal $4M gross profit $1.5M*

Sales executive #3: *Actual volume $3.5M assigned yearly goal $2.5M gross profit $1M*

Junior sales associate: *Actual volume $3.25M assigned yearly goal $1.8M gross profit $1.5M*

In this scenario, our junior sales associate is not far away from sales executive #1. Junior is only $500,000 away on profitability with $1.75M less in overall volume! Nice job to the newbie!

Also, sales executive #2 needs a path for correction since numbers like those could have you looking for a new job, unfortunately, even though the profit is considerable. Being $1.5M off from the assigned yearly goal could mean either the accounts or opportunities simply do not match the goals being set. Or it could be that #2 is just not that good. The facts here are that something will change at some point. Who makes the *change is a different story, and any good sales leader will keep a close eye on their upcoming performance in the next few months. Lots of luck, #2!*

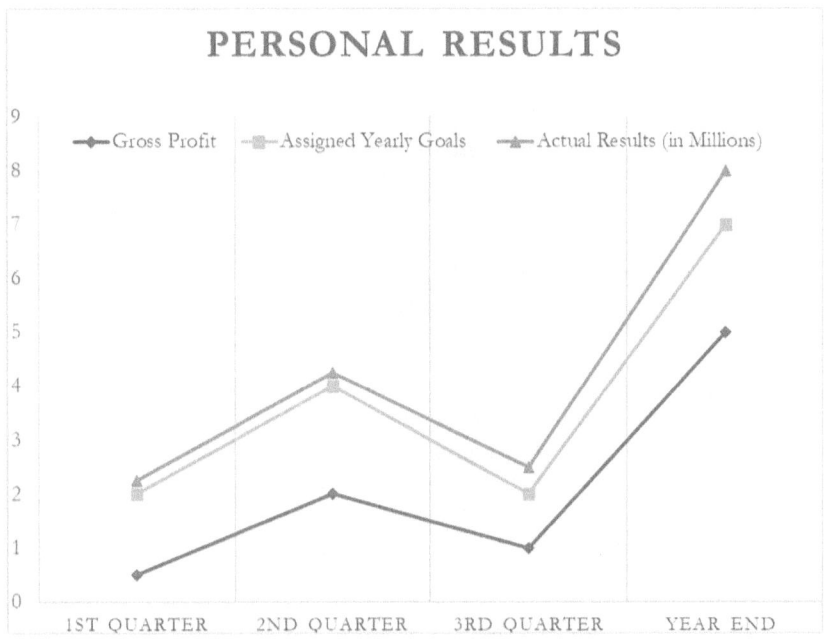

PERSONAL RESULTS

—◆—Gross Profit   —■—Assigned Yearly Goals   —▲—Actual Results (in Millions)

In the line chart above, you have sales results for an individual seller. This graph is perfect for a one-on-one with your manager or simply to use as your own tracker. These results are typical, and if this is how yours looks, nice job! Why this chart looks like this can be for many reasons, but here are a few typical reasons as to why. It is a slow season for the industry you're in, traditionally the third quarter for whatever reason. You may have been very excited about your second-quarter results that you had just a few extra days off, long lunches, or lack of motivation. We have all been there, and as always, "the numbers don't lie." And don't think your boss doesn't see that. It's important to maintain your constant drive, determination, and aggressive nature in order to move those results and profit lines upward!

This example shows healthy results, along with the profit that tracks as it should. This sales leader that set these goals truly knows this seller. The goal tracks with results and profit. This example shows this seller had a very strong fourth quarter which may indicate that some projects were also held aside for some time. Or maybe those companies had extra funds that needed to be spent in order to get them back the following calendar year—either way, very strong performance to close the year! Maybe that large project that took you six months to research, qualify, hold countless meetings and conference calls over finally sold. Good for you!

All the effort you put into it shows clearly. Now be careful. It's recorded as a sale with you as the seller. Next year, the boss very well may expect those same types of results again! You say it isn't possible, but the sales leader may very well say find it somewhere! Most leaders do understand there is such a thing as a "one-hit wonder." So you most likely will not get that entire revenue of this big project sold into your goals for the following year, but certainly, a good 50 percent should be! Here is a hint, your boss may have known that project was going to sell. Look at the year-end assigned goal! They didn't become the boss by chance.

WHY TOP PERFORMERS ARE PENALIZED WITH SALES GOALS

USUALLY, AN ORGANIZATION will count on one or two key sales professionals every year. These are the people that no matter what the economy is doing, no matter what someone in the past has tried to sell and couldn't, this person can. That is a blessing and a curse. They're making good money and are looked upon as the "top guns." Now they're also carrying the majority of the burden for the sales goals. I've never seen a company lower the sales targets for the year. So as they go up annually, someone has to carry the majority of this increase. Usually, it's that person or team on top.

As the top performer, you may feel this goal is insignificant. To you, it means nothing since you know you will beat it. If this is your mindset, good for you! Nothing will stop you from achieving this, and you're a true professional! Or you're just lucky enough to have all of the larger accounts in your office. However, this could still wear down many people that have this burden every year. Just have faith, continue to do what you do, singles and doubles, and take it one sale at a time. You know in your heart you will get there! Don't look at the annual goal. Look at it one transaction at a time. Monthly, look at the overall and gauge where you are to adapt your habits accordingly.

Top performers are usually the ones that have outlived many transient managers, coworkers, and company restructuring efforts. To them, they don't care so much about what's going on around them. Their sole interest is bringing in that new business. However, as I've seen in many cases, these are also the people the fulfillment team complains about the most. The "top gun" in some cases doesn't care about equipment delays, time lines, manpower shortages, etc. He or she cares about one thing, getting the next order and making sure they're on top. This is not a team player or someone you want to be! Top performer, yes, but be a team player always!

Here is why you need balance regarding the above paragraph. Even though they're driving business for the company, they should not be making others around them miserable. Now your company needs this person to drive sales, but sometimes, that can get out of balance. As the top performer, you also need to consider your fulfillment/execution team and what you're selling and promising to your customer. You still need to engage those teams of people as I've mentioned. You should be staying involved to assist where needed to ensure your customer gets what was promised and at the agreed deadline. Remember what I stated earlier that you need one another. The acquisition and fulfillment teams must live together in this business climate. This mindset and drive will help keep you at the top of the pack!

Don't forget to give back to your industry. Take on the new trainee and have them do your small tasks. Show them the way and provide a clear path to what has helped drive your personal success. Some tenured people would think I'm crazy for suggesting that since it would give away the "secret recipe" of their selling style. Invest in that person, and they will always be an advocate for you. This will pay off someday. The time investment in them initially will help keep you at the top. Once trained, that will allow you additional customer face time to do what we do. Then once they want more and become a junior sales associate, rinse and repeat with the next NUG! Teach, help, mentor, give back, reinvest in your industry, and who knows, that NUG could be your boss someday!

MANAGING PEOPLE

AS A PERSON that has spent many years in a sales role, you may feel like getting into management. There's nothing wrong with this, but there are some things to consider.

As the sales manager, you're truly responsible for driving all sales of your team/company. Here are some duties of the typical sales manager:

- Supervise your sales team and their day-to-day activity.
- Supervise opportunities they're pursuing and make sure all areas of the project are covered.
- Provide assistance when they struggle with pricing, specifications of a bid, clarifications, etc.
- You need to be the mediator when difficulties occur with a potential new customer.
- Provide a pipeline of opportunities for your team to keep them motivated and driven to sell.
- Most likely, you're responsible for all financials of your team and the company sales targets.
- When sales rep A calls on sales rep B's customer, you will referee that issue for sure.
- Salespeople are pushy, opinionated, and driven. Have fun dealing with those attitudes daily.
- When a sales rep is not on plan and not making their quotas, you need to coach to correction.

- When a new talented junior sales rep is hired, you need to design an assimilation/growth plan.
- Many times, you will need to be the visionary of the company, where to drive future sales efforts.
- You must mentor your team, guide them, and assist in their success. This builds respect.
- Being there when they need you is a big part of being a leader. Always make time for your team.

Here is a big one for you, usually the sales manager makes less than the high-performing sales executives/professionals. A decent salary is usually a standard, so you don't have to worry about paying the bills. Typically, they're bonus eligible based on growth, so you want your people to sell, which helps your bonus potential. That's where the big financial kickers come into play. I've known sales leaders that could make tens of thousands of dollars each quarter when their team exceeded revenue targets!

Of course, any sales leadership role will have benefits and drawbacks. But being there for the team when they have issues regardless of what they are is very important—one of the biggest parts of being a good and respected leader in my opinion.

If you have a sales executive that has issues at home with a spouse, kids, bills, etc., how effective will they be at work? How effective will they be in front of customers? I can say, not very effective or driven to succeed. Their mind is in a completely different universe. You need course correction and fast! Of course, you're not a therapist, but at times, figure it out! They need you, the company needs you, and the annual sales targets need you.

If you do this, they won't forget it. They will drive harder since they know that you were there when they needed you! You will build a stronger relationship with that person, and then when praise is spoken about you, don't blow it off or feel embarrassed. Simply say thanks! Yes, it's part of your job, but that's a well-earned perk. Good job, boss!

When I was a sales leader (upcoming chapter), I had a top-performing commercial HVAC account manager that reported to me. This was our "top gun" that always had a pipeline of opportunities, sold the most on our team, and did well for himself. However, when his mother's disease progressed, I lost him. He was traveling to see her almost daily, which was a day trip, so no big deal, right? That is until his aggressive sales nature was lost and rightly so since he was focused on her. This sounds bad, but stay with me. I still had a dozen or so install-ers and technicians that needed work. How would they stay on the payroll if we didn't have a healthy pipeline? I spent time with him after hours, talking about his mother, watching him break down, listening to him say to me that his mother no longer recognized him, horrible to hear. But I had to support him as a man, his leader, and friend.

Unfortunately, his mother did eventually pass away. She didn't suffer long, and he was at peace with the fact that she was at rest. He did thank me for the time we spent together and for listening. I can't tell you the dividends that paid when several months later, I told him that our pipeline was low. Within days, he pulled through with a few hundred thousand dollars of new work for the company. A team member, partner, coworker, and friend—talk about a relationship!

It isn't directing or leading people in the direction you want them to go in. It's going as a team in the direction you all want to drive toward. See the difference? *It's being "a boss" or a "leader they will work hard for and always remember."* Look at it this way, a dictator tells their people what to do, say, how to act, sometimes what to even wear. Crazy—but some leaders are simply telling their sales professionals what to sell, how to sell, what to say, and how to do it. If that's the style of your manager or someone you know, I'm not discrediting them. It's a style, just not mine.

My style as you may have gathered at this point was more of a team member that people can relate to, someone that has been in their shoes and someone that wants to drive business as a team. The respect will be gained much quicker than most with this approach. When you meet as a team, have an open discussion on vision, prod-ucts/offerings, how to do it, and what the strategy will be, that's team-work and a winning culture. The team collectively buys into what we're all doing. Certainly, the inmates will not run the asylum, and you need to put borders in place, but empowering the team together for the same vision is powerful, and something I really enjoyed.

MY DAYS IN MANAGEMENT

AFTER EARNING MANY sales awards and good money for several years, I started to think differently. I really enjoyed helping and teaching, always did! Back when I was a senior field technician, I loved the times when our field leader Rob would say, "Hey, Joe, we have a new technician starting tomorrow. Take him for a week, see what you think, and let me know how he does," or when I had an intern assigned to me when I was a senior sales executive—showing someone fresh out of college what it takes to investigate opportunities, price-complex projects, deal with subcontractors, reading prospects/customers, and the biggest one, how to build relationships. So after all those years and just a few simple examples I just provided, I figured it was time and the most logical step for a new chapter in my career.

I was recruited away from my company and a seventeen-year tenure. It was a very hard decision since many of these coworkers were friends and watched me mature. They were at my wedding, saw my wife and I start to raise two daughters, but it was time. I needed to take this new opportunity and grow as a professional. The job offer was great, and I just couldn't pass on it.

So there I was at a new company. I was a new employee with a big position that was two under the president! Now what was I to do? I had eight residential/commercial HVAC sales executives, two field installation managers, and another dozen or more field installers and technicians under my leadership—in total, twenty-seven, all while being a new leader! But I knew I could do it and always liked a challenge!

Things were flying past me for the first month or two, but I held tight! Now I was understanding the company processes, the structure, and most importantly, all the different personalities. I had a large sales target assigned on my team from my first day. It truly was sink or swim! Our company president would often travel, leaving the general manager in charge. Well, that person also liked to take days off, so that left me as the go-to for issues, and they always happened when those two were away. I swear I thought they made them up to test me! But, of course, they didn't, and I was then responsible for another forty or so people and several hundred customers. I loved the power and the responsibility.

As the months went on, I helped my teams grow. I built some very solid relationships that years later, I still have. I made a lot of changes and was proud to see my ideas grow and mature to make the company a better place. But I felt like an HR manager! I found myself daily dealing with "He said, she said," angry customers, and worst of all, hiring and firing—interviewing sales or technical people, making job offers, building assimilation plans and job descriptions… blah blah. It was really boring and wearing me out.

The typical workday was extremely long. I would be in the office usually by about 6:30 a.m. to help get the install crews ready to get on the road to be at a home or business for a start time of roughly 8:00 a.m. I would usually be in the office until the same time of about 6:30, just p.m. I dealt mostly with the business overall during the day, along with commercial customer's questions, issues, etc. Well, after about 6:00 p.m., the phone would ring with the residential complaints, questions, or concerns. The homeowners were also needing support on many weekends. So the sales executives and team leaders would escalate to me with those concerns. It truly was a job that never ended. No false promises were made to me either. I knew my role and what needed to be done.

My homelife was upside down. I never saw my two daughters, and when I was home, I was on the phone with an issue. My wife also put in ten- or eleven-hour days and certainly didn't want to hear my phone ring and ring. It got to a point where I would keep it in my pocket on silent mode all weekend, talk about never disconnecting from the office! But it was a high-level role with a good paycheck, so it was my choice to live that way. I knew this was what it took in order to be good at this job!

At first, when I came home after a day that spanned about twelve hours, my girls would scream, "Daddy's home," and run up to me and hug my legs. It was the best part of my day! Well, after about six months, their reaction to my arrival that late in the day started to fade. I even asked my wife one night as I stood right inside by the front door and said, "They don't even come up to me anymore and greet me." Her reply was "Well, Joe, they're just used to you not being around anymore." I will never forget that conversation. It wasn't said in a derogatory way. It was the truth but hard to digest—something had to give and soon.

The worst was the firing. When it was warranted, it was easy. Cut and dry as they say! But when the company had to reduce manpower, those layoffs were bad but for the greater good of the company overall. Looking someone in the face and telling them that today is their last day is a gut-wrenching ugly thing to do—having a grown man or woman break down in front of you and ask how they will make their rent or mortgage, having someone with a new baby at home, knowing they're already somewhat struggling, but I had to let them go! So I asked to have them sent to my office. That news traveled fast! I had tremendous respect for the president of that company. I certainly didn't envy or want his job!

The absolute worst thing for me more so than the above examples was the person-to-person interaction. I lost that with many people in the company. If they saw me walking down the hall, they would turn and go another direction. Really? I was always the fun guy that wanted to help everyone, drive business for the company, and make money. What happened? I became the guy that no one wanted to be called by and certainly not asked into my office. I didn't like that, but again, I chose this. I wanted a big role with responsibility. Nothing was hidden, and the role was fully transparent before I took it.

I realized this when on a Monday I would hear something like "Hey, Joe, can I speak with you for a minute?" then I heard, "We need to reduce head count, so have it done by Friday." You see, at this point, I had fired all the bad employees with attitudes, the ones that always let us down when we needed them most, always called out on a Monday or Friday, and just weren't team players. These firings I had to do now were hard. These were decisions that kept me up half the night, came with tightness in my chest, and gave me just constant worry and anxiety. It was business, not personal. I was in a high-level role with a lot of responsibility. So it was my job and what I was hired to do. The company knew what I was doing was difficult, but again, it had to be done. It was just business, and I was being compensated well to do it. I don't ever want to own my own business, glamorous it certainly is not.

So take your pick—all good workers, all did what is asked of them and more, all have families, all come to work with a smile, and all have the customer's best interest at heart. It was crazy times for me personally, along with many gray hairs mysteriously starting to appear. I knew I couldn't live this way much longer. It would either put me in the hospital or land me in divorce court since situations like these, you just take home and live with.

To lighten the mood here, I also had a few funny firings. I would like to share the stories about employee #1 and employee #2. Now let me start off by saying they're both very happy now! Employee #1 has grown within our industry and is doing well, and #2 finished college and is with a big global company. Okay, so don't think I am a sociopath for chuckling as I write.

Employee #1 just wasn't doing well with our company. Someone else hired him, and I took him into our department. He was not good in front of customers and wasn't grasping the many policies we had as a larger professional company. But the tardiness, absences, customer complaints, etc. just seemed to follow him around. Our company culture was one of being better than the rest. I was proud of that. Unfortunately, he needed to work for one of those other companies.

So he had to go, and one of my managers went looking for him in the building. Where did he go? Well, he was hiding in one of the

117

stalls in the bathroom. Someone told him that I needed him in my office. He would not come out! You see, this is what I was talking about! I had to go and tell him to get out of the stall since he wouldn't budge! I think he might have had a few other underlying things going on, and it was best for the company that he be released. When I said the words "Today is your last day with our company," he started crying and asking how he would take care of his dog! Meanwhile, this is a young man, maybe twenty-two that lived with his parents. I'm sure the dog was just fine!

Employee #2 was a big-hearted guy that I really enjoyed working with. He is one of those that just grew on you over time. But he always seemed to make his mouth get him in trouble, and I would try to coach him on his comments or e-mail replies. He also had a liking for those double or triple burgers from the fast-food chains. So he loved to eat that stuff and hear our reactions as to why it was not good for him. Of course, I would tell him as others would that we cared about him and his health. I also would tell him to come to lunch with me and have some healthier foods, and, of course, he would laugh.

Well, one day, #2 said something that could not be taken back. I had to bring him into the general manager's office, and I figured I would get that special pre-orchestrated look and would have to let him go. I didn't want to do that and told him before we went into the office that if I tap your foot with mine, that means to close your lips! Well, what do you think he did? He voiced himself too much, and, of course, the look was given, and I had to let him go.

The funny part here is this: when I was walking him out of the building, I said, "I wish you well. You're a smart guy and friend, and I know you will have success. But next time you want to pick up one of those burgers, think of me telling you not to do it!" Well, that was all it took. He grabbed me in a bear hug, pulled me into him, and was emotional. Not only did he sob all over me, but also he screamed, "You really care about me!" over and over and repeating that line! He was a smart guy that knew his job well, but I just couldn't mentor him enough to change his business habits.

Again, he is very successful now, and he told me a short time afterward that I was too good to be at that company. Ironically, I was thinking that for the past few months but never told anyone. How was he that in tune with me? How did he know what I was already thinking? He used to say that he could read people very well. He also said that he had a keen sense of what people are made of. I guess he did after all. A funny and good guy, I really enjoyed working alongside him.

So I did make a lot of changes for the better. I did hire many good people. I did make the company money, but worst of all, I had to let some really good people go. Again, it was my job that I signed up for. It wasn't for me any longer, and I knew my life at home and work needed to get back into balance. So I officially resigned shortly thereafter and went to a global competitor back in a sales professional role, one of the best career moves I've ever made to go back! Many years later, I still have zero desire to get back into a management or a sales leadership position.

This chapter is not to deter anyone from moving up the corporate ladder into a leadership position. I learned a great deal and believe it or not, very grateful for that opportunity and the knowledge I gained working there. It's simply to outline my time of two years in that type of leadership role and also to provide some humor in some sad situations I experienced as a leader.

WORK-LIFE BALANCE IN SALES

I DID MENTION in the beginning of the book that getting into sales had its freedoms, but I wanted to elaborate below.

There are way too many things to juggle between our life at home which may or may not include a spouse, kids, family pet, sports, school activities, and several other things. Then we deal with our workload, quotas, deadlines, and meetings internal and external with customers! How does a sales professional deal with all of it? I can say from experience, you will have a much easier time than most.

For example, my wife works the corporate job day in and day out, doing the commute, the traffic, the countless hours behind a desk, meetings, interviews, presentations, and that's only to name what she does by noon! If she's lucky, she's able to leave her desk and go to her cafeteria for a sandwich. Sound like a job you want? I would hope you would say, "No way!" But most people live that life five to six days a week. We all wonder why so many in our country have high blood pressure, ulcers, stress, anxiety, and whatever else you can imagine. Then they simply pop pills that the doctor prescribed.

Sales professionals are more unique in how we have the ability to work. Many of us are able to get the kids from school or make that doctor's appointment during the day. Most of us have the ability to work remotely, many times from a home office if you're lucky enough to invest in one. In my opinion, if you don't have one, get one! Buy an inexpensive desk, filing cabinet, printer, and another monitor/computer to make the workday easier. By doing this, no commute and no wasted time at the "watercooler," talking about last night's ball game. Of course, there's time to do that, and you should bond with coworkers. But think of the productivity you can pick up by not having all the external things that distract us!

We also can make dinner for the family, get the kids to their game or school concert that night. Then later, once the house quiets down, you can close the door to your home office or in my case, the basement door and catch up on estimates or proposals. As long as you're diligent about this, there really shouldn't be an issue with your boss. You must commit that time back to work which is very important. I admit, sometimes early in my career, it was hard. But over time, the rhythm and cadence were built. The more time you spend estimating and proposing, the higher chance you have to sell more work, meet and exceed your quota, and make additional income…win-win! Plant those seeds by getting more proposals out, secure more face-to-face meetings, and follow up on projects already bid. These are all things that can be done by working from home, at night or on a random weekend afternoon.

Many sales managers also don't want their teams sitting in an office. They do want you on the road, in meetings, doing customer lunches, dinners, company-sponsored events, and things such as this. Remember, as I said earlier, these are all relationship builders. Those are what your career should be based on. The boss also knows that when salespeople get together, nothing gets accomplished! They brag about that huge sale, the new TV show, baseball or football game, or anything else but sales.

That's why sales leaders usually know to keep their teams full of opportunities, help them drive business, and keep them out of the office sitting behind their desk! My point to all this is simple. In sales, you can have that flexibility to have a good balance and not be in the grind like my poor wife Jennifer. You can work late at night or a weekend occasionally to get a proposal out to a customer (yes, you do call them within the next day or two and try to schedule a meeting in person), weekends are ideal also and hear me out before you say no! When you're relaxing watching a game, open the laptop and work on an estimate. When you have the young kids down for a nap, finish up a proposal. When you're up after everyone has gone to bed, plan out your next day or week of meetings and tighten that forecast. Use all your time as efficiently as possible to maximize success!

In sales, it isn't time spent behind a desk and watching the clock until it displays 5:00 p.m. or better, not trying to be the first one out the door either! It is time utilization—how to work, what to work on, and wherever you do it from doesn't matter! *Your time and relationships are some of the most valuable things in all of sales that you have control over.*

REASONS FOR WRITING

IN MY CURRENT role, I've traveled all around the country for business. I have spent way too many hours delayed in airports, on planes, eating alone at a restaurant, and wide awake at 3 a.m. in a strange hotel. My point is this, I simply started to write down discussion points during those periods of time of possible chapters, then one page became five, ten, etc. All of what has been written here has truly taken several years. I hope I was able to guide you toward a solid foundation in sales as a rookie. Believe in yourself since you are your biggest fan. Work hard, learn, listen more than you speak, and always do what you say you will. Stay the course, and good solid efforts will be rewarded over time!

If you're a veteran of this craft, I hope I was able to spark memories of things you've accomplished in years past, opened your mind to think differently, and potentially, I've given you an advantage in closing more business. I also respect anyone with a tenured career in sales. Believe me, I know it isn't easy!

I've also spoken about what has worked very well for me in my career—the different stages of a sales professional's career, how to find opportunities, partner with people to succeed, work smart and not hard. I spoke about where to spend your time, opportunity qualifying, and how to mature and adapt with your own strategic vision. But the biggest thing I want to get across here is relationships. Those are the things that should be cherished above all. Working with people that you truly enjoy and want to be with is a blessing. *Find the good in everyone that you work with.* Always have that smile and be that role model to the junior people and a strong partner for the tenured. Bond with those coworkers and customers alike. *Look at yourself in that mirror and be proud of what you see!* Don't undercut your fellow sales teams in order to steal a sale. Don't talk poorly about a coworker and be that negative person. People like that enjoy the negative and draw others in to mimic their behavior. Stay away. You're better than that!

I truly enjoy coaching and watching others grow. I owe that as a veteran to anyone entering into a sales career. If that person comes into my life and wants my input, I'm happy to help. I've been told in the past that my words were "nuggets" to the younger generation. A junior salesperson would take that nugget or tidbit of information, put it in their pocket, and keep it for their career. A few of the junior sales reps would call them "Joe's nuggets" or say that my "nuggets" were in their pocket. You can take that as you will (insert smiley face here).

But watching someone grow professionally and having something to do with their success is almost as much enjoyment as watching a child hit a home run or score the winning goal. For me, it's true enjoyment, and I'm blessed to feel as I do when teaching or guiding someone in their career. That's probably the biggest driver for writing, being able to share my stories across a large platform and helping someone else succeed.

Soar high in the clouds like an eagle way above the negativity. Good people are drawn to other good people. Strong, intelligent, and successful people can sense others alike. Be them. Join them even if you don't belong initially. They will accept you. Learn and become them. Listen more than you talk. Good people help and encourage other good people. Eagles soar with other eagles!

Cherish the relationships you build at work and at home. Encourage and support one another. Have a good attitude and positive outlook always. Be the best husband, father, wife, mother, partner, coworker, and friend that you can be. If for some reason that day you failed, then tomorrow do your best, apologize, and start fresh! Sales is what we do, but being the absolute best person you can be wins any day. *Please remember the personal legacy you're building. Encourage and empower. Love and be understanding. I truly wish you all the success I've had so far in my career, but I only wish you more!*

Now listen here, you sales pro, no more reading. Get off your butt! Get out there and go sell something!

ABOUT THE AUTHOR

AS A CHILD of a working-class divorced household, we struggled to get by. I found that having fun, playing sports, and landing in typical teenager trouble were more important than working hard in the classroom. As an athlete, I was offered a college scholarship, but being in a classroom for another four years just wasn't for me.

A guidance counselor said a technical trade would be a great option, and many paid well. Here I was, eighteen and in a technical institute, learning HVAC (heating, ventilation, and air-conditioning). I dedicated the next two years to studying, working hard, and learning the basics of a wonderful industry that I'm still involved with thirty years later!

I spent fourteen years after graduation in the HVAC field as a technician, working on large commercial and industrial applications and eventually transitioned into a junior sales role. The hard work ethic continued as the years passed. Sales was providing me with a comfortable life. I was truly blessed with financial and job security, year after year earning "Top Gun in Sales," "Annual Quota Breaker," or "Elite Club" awards.

Now the sales part of my career has spanned more than fifteen years, and the gratitude can't be quantified! The main reason for writing is to allow people entering into any sales role or for a sales veteran to learn from my experiences. I've excelled in my craft, worked hard, built relationships, and been a top performer for years. The awards and achievements are many, and I'm lucky to have this platform to share my knowledge and experience.

A very special thanks to Kevin, Joe, Connor, Yao and Mounica. You all were my inspiration for writing. Watching each of you grow and knowing I had a small part in that is so very humbling. I wish you the best and continued success!

To Frank and Mike, I can't thank you both enough for your guidance throughout my career. I'm confident in saying that much of my success is because both of you were mentors in my life! Frank, you helped drive me toward a sales career and coached me every step of the way in my early years. Mike, you refined my skills many years later, selling to high-level executives. You, guys, are like my work-fathers and will always have a special place in my life!

To my family, Jennifer, Allison, and Olivia, I do what I do for the three of you. Well, and for Logan also. We always joke and say that something always happens at home when I'm traveling for work. Whether it's missing Allison hitting the walk-off double to win the softball game, being away for Olivia's music concert, or poor Jenn cutting her finger on a tuna can and getting stitches while I'm at a dinner meeting in Virginia! Things like this always seem to transpire time and time again when I'm away. So for any future mishaps, let me publicly apologize here for all to read…haha.

Thank you for always being so supportive and understanding. I love you guys.

www.ingramcontent.com/pod-product-compliance
Lightning Source LLC
Chambersburg PA
CBHW021435210526
45463CB00002B/522